GOD
MADE ME
WAIT!

Pray, Plan & Write Your Forever

By: Sherrell Duncan *&* Natasha T. Brown

Printed in the United States of America
For permissions requests or bulk orders contact Brown & Duncan Brand at
connect@BandDBrand.com.

Scripture quotations are from the New King James Version®.
Copyright©1982 by Thomas Nelson. Used by permission. All rights
reserved.

Cover photography by Brian Dickerson and Katisha Smittick of Mental
Mayhem Photography
Book cover design by Brown & Duncan Brand, LLC.
Typeset design by All-En Virtual Solutions

ISBN: 978-0-9984756-0-8

Editor's Review

This book is a beautiful, openhearted account of two journeys to self-acceptance, peace, and a trusting reliance on the love of God that will make readers seek Him like never before. Natasha and Sherrell are so refreshingly real and raw in their storytelling, and they openly and fearlessly share some of the most intimate, significant stories of their lives. I cheered with them, cried for them, and was just touched by their willingness to be so courageous and true. In their experiences, women will see some part of themselves, their own vulnerabilities, and their strength. God Make Me Wait, to me, is about those critical life conversations that women need to have, but don't get—aren't getting—anywhere else. Every woman who reads this will be so grateful. I definitely am.

- Stefanie Manns

Contents

"He who is without sin among you, let him throw a stone at her first."
- Jesus (John 8:7)

Introduction

When I met "Sherrella La Bella" in 2009, I was a "sweet," young professional in my twenties, who had just completed a master's degree program at Towson University. I was starting a communications agency and preparing to move back to the DMV. I was egotistical, conceited, and addicted to things (that I'll describe in detail later), and searching for the fast life. I was working full-time as a development communications associate at a boarding school in rural Pennsylvania. I came home to the DMV every chance I could! I had also just ended a five-year relationship, with a woman, and I had jumped right into an on-again-off again "friends with benefits" situation with a local rapper and dope dealer, who happened to be Sherrell's client with her company, Honeycomb Set. I was nine months into my "new life" of being single, dating, and was ready to launch my business and show the world that I was a boss.

I actually found Sherrell on Facebook. She tagged the dude who was "off again" by this time, in a post that went to his timeline. This of course raised my jealous antennas, and I went snooping around on her page and through their "Facebook Friendship." To my surprise, I found an outgoing, well-connected female boss, who seemed like someone that I needed to know. So I hit her up via the Facebook Messenger and told her that I wanted to connect. She invited me to an event that she was having the following week, and the rest was history.

1

I was planning for my biggest event as the creator of Honeycomb Set. It was a lot of pressure because I was hosting it right in the heart of downtown DC at a museum. No one had ever used the spot like I was about to use it. It was a "must-see" event. My driving force was unfortunately to show my ex that I could do exactly what he did, only better. My goal was to win, to make him look like he was losing. It was a horrible way to look at (or define) success, but it sure did help my motivation at that time. The show was also on my 25th birthday, so we had to make it huge. I connected with some old friends from my old neighborhood in Riverdale, and we produced the event. They took over the after party situation, and I was in charge of the show.

The show's format was genius (there would be fashion and music performances from some of the hottest local rappers) and the whole DMV was catching wind of it. The promotion of the event drew a lot of people in, including the likes of Natasha T. Brown. I will never forget the first day I met her. She was so bubbly and full of life. She wasn't the average chick I would kick it with, but I definitely wanted to do business with her, because she was so BAWSE! She pulled up in a black Range Rover and got out with this beautiful mane of hair down her back, and I was like, "Yep, it's on." I felt it in my spirit that we were about to kill the game. We met. We talked. We drank. We bonded. We connected. It was the beginning of an everlasting friendship.

If God is making you wait, realize that often times, you may actually be the cause. Perhaps your heart or character isn't where God wants it. He will make us wait to prepare our hearts and character for the work He wants to accomplish through us. At other times, He wants to check our motives: waiting often weeds out the real things from the facade. At one point, in pre-marital class, Pastor James Marshall asked the class the following question: Why do you want to be married? Is it because you want to post the ring on social media or you want to be a "Mrs?" Either way, God knows your true motives, so He may be making you "wait" to transform your heart.

The wait may also be a "divine delay" designed for the Glory of God, similar to what happened in John 11, when Jesus raised Lazarus from the dead. Although Jesus knew that Lazarus was sick, He waited two days to go to him, and by the time Jesus arrived, Lazarus had been dead for four days. This "wait" however served a purpose. By the time Jesus arrived, the neighbors and townspeople had all gathered to console Martha and Mary. This scene set the perfect stage for Jesus to perform a miracle or sign that would cause others to believe in Him. God also makes us wait because He is preparing the atmosphere. Or perhaps He's still preparing us or those who He wants us to unite with. Regardless of the reason for the wait, the key is to trust God, pray to Him, and begin praising Him during your season of preparation. As you wait, remember that God withholds no good thing from those who love Him. He always has our very best in store. So you can trust Him.

Back then, our view of success, relationships, and God were warped and dysfunctional. We had no clue that our thinking was off-base and our mindsets were toxic, which of course seeped out through our actions. We based our values on the world's values, despite both having relationships with God. We lived in the moment, without considering the lasting effects of our actions. We had little-to-no boundaries in our personal lives, and a woman without boundaries leaves herself open to predators of all types. While the stories and prayers that follow are from Natasha and Sherrell, the "we" in this book is inclusive of the women we've met from around the world, who are in search of peace, bound by past pain, tired of their current circumstances, and are ready to thrive in their God-given purpose. So many of us live life ashamed of our past, in bondage of our transgressions, and afraid to share our stories. When these women (and men) come to the church, they often find that their problems are even too *taboo* for "Christians" to touch. This is one reason why there are so many people who run from religion and relationship with God. Religious people scare others in our generation away. The reason is, many religious people are often legalistic just as the Pharisees were in the bible. They are condemning, uncompromising, not relatable, judgmental, and disconnected from "the world" so much that they cannot relate to people in the world. (FYI, we love God, but we have abandoned religion for relationship and we'd encourage you to do the same.) We are here to demonstrate how real and uncut our relationships with God can get. Perhaps you can relate to some of the scenes that follow and the toxic circumstances that we've overcome. You'll read how we made ourselves slaves to the world: the partying, the drinking, the hustling, the sex, and the toxic relationships. Finally, we hit rock bottom. For many women who were once caught up by the world and Satan's deception, "rock bottom" actually becomes our saving grace where we are re-introduced to Jesus, and become awakened to God's ultimate purpose for our lives.

God Made Me Wait is a transformational process of the bads and goods. We were so bad, and while we share these experiences here, in an effort to help you face your own demons, we are in no way glorifying our sin. We must, however "keep it real," for lack of a better term. Keeping it real is often made to sound like the easiest thing to do, but in fact, it's one of the hardest - and boldest statements that we can make. Our keeping it real is gutter and gross at times. You may be prompted to turn up your nose, and begin to judge us as so many others would have done had they known the truth. As public figures, who at this point were both quite influential in our region and respective industries, we learned how to hide the truth and present the public with only the image that they needed to see or that we wanted everyone to see. Today, however, perpetrating for the public seems like the norm. We live in the age of filters and selfies, and our social media friends must only see the pretty angels, the perfect hair days, and the videos and snapshots of the high moments of our lives - even if those high moments are fabricated and haunted by abuse, addiction, feelings of worthlessness, and a lack of self-care.

So many of us, as women, don't love ourselves.

So many of us validate our worth by likes on social media.

So many of us stay with partners that are bad for us, because we don't want to be alone.

So many of us place our worth on our success or how successful we are at manipulating men (or situations).

We devalue ourselves.

We underestimate ourselves.

We play into what society says is right, good, beautiful, and worthy.

And we deceive ourselves with lies that God never approved or intended for us to accept.

If you have never fallen victim to any of these circumstances, good for you. We encourage you to close this book now, and give it to your daughter, good-good girlfriend, prayer partner, or sister, who have no doubt been waiting for someone to be honest about what she too has been facing.

We decided to write this book to honor God and demonstrate to you the power of our almighty Father to work wonders in any of our lives, even *when* we are a HOT MESS. We were that hot mess, and you will most likely agree as you meet our former selves. Even at the point in which we met, although we were positive and productive on the outside, neither of us knew the demons that the other was really battling. Not until we began to have transparent moments, in between meetings and photo shoots, were we able to let our guards down and truly become *real* friends. Before we met each other, a similar set of circumstances had shaped our hearts and spirits to discern that we should connect. Although many of these circumstances were negative, they led us to each other, and we managed to always produce positive results for the public, be it a charitable initiative, women's empowerment event, or media production. God does work all things together for the good of those who love Him and are called according to His purpose. (Romans 8:28) So please, whatever you do, no matter how bad it gets, don't stop loving HIM!

At one point, though, we both crashed. Sherrell had a baby, found herself suffering with postpartum depression, which she tried to relieve through alcohol and food. And as a result, she gained nearly 100 pounds, and topped the scale at close to 300 pounds, causing her to have a mild heart attack and nearly die! Natasha's insecurities, need to feel loved, and reliance on physical attributes and superficial qualities in men, landed her in a relationship that nearly took her life. She endured almost three years of domestic violence, along with a broken nose, broken ribs, gashed forehead, bite marks, and more. Her *hell* climaxed once she was wrongfully accused of trying to kill her abuser. Though we wish these tragedies on no one, we do pray that everyone reading this gets a wakeup call if necessary. We both had our own crosses to bear, and since the moment we met, God has been the centerpiece that brought us to the other to speak life when life was so desperately needed. And what an amazing work of our almighty God to keep this friendship alive, once we both stepped into our purpose. This is crucial, because as humans, we often grow apart from those who we hung with in our sin, once we come to know and commit our lives to Christ.

Thankfully, this was not true for us, and even through distance, months without communication, and no superficial validation from the other, we continued to love each other through our mess, tests, tragedies, and now, God-given strategies. We praised God so much after Sherrell was surprised with a dream engagement and wedding all in the same day. We didn't expect God to take this union to a global platform, but we are so honored and thankful that He did. We know that through Alfred and Sherrell's union, God is putting true love and obedience on blast. But He is also demonstrating His power to TRANSFORM. We thank God that He had transformed the hearts of us two authors, and that He linked us in friendship years prior so that Natasha could serve as brand manager for this amazing movement! How awesome is it that when Sherrell's proposal and marriage were placed on an international platform, Natasha had already been thriving as a bestselling author and Christian ghostwriter? God does not make any mistakes at all.

GOD MADE ME WAIT!

And as Sherrell would always say, *it is already written!*

God Made Me Wait is for you, if you've been through something and now you're willing to wait on God for your next move. We want to help you. We know it's not easy to wait on God and it's so simple to become distracted, however, one of the main points of us telling our stories, sharing our prayers, and inviting you into daily devotion and journaling is to encourage you to communicate to God even through your mess. That's what we did. We sinned. We talked to God. We fought with and staked out boyfriends, yet we did not deny God's ability to transform our hearts. At points we were suicidal, and yet that did not keep us from calling out the name of God. The writings that follow are from our personal prayer journals. We compiled these prayers and stories, our favorite scriptures, and devotionals just for you.

Remember that God answers every prayer. Sometimes the answer is yes, sometimes it is no, and sometimes, more often than we'd like, the answer is WAIT.

In Mark 2:17, Jesus said, *"I did not come to call the righteous, but sinners, to repentance."*

We pray that the intimate and transparent moments that we shared with God, even in our mess, give you strength and hope. We encourage you to read through these pages with an open heart, an open mind, and an attitude of grace. Romans 8:1 says *Therefore, there is now no condemnation for those of us who are in Christ Jesus.* So if you can relate to the sins we committed, then we know you can relate to the God that we're committed to. There is no condemnation for you, only redemption and transformation. We can freely admit and share these confessions and prayers with you, and we pray that you too are just as honest and naked before God, so that He can truly transform your heart and life the way He has ours. We declare blessings for you as you wait in expectancy for God to elevate you to a place that you have yet to imagine.

With love,

Sherrell & Natasha

Part 1

PRAY.

Even in your mess.

You've kept track of my every toss and turn
through the sleepless nights,
Each tear entered in your ledger,
each ache written in your book.
Psalms 56:8 (MSG)

Let us paint a picture for you of what life was like before we committed our lives and hearts to Christ. You ever watch a movie and there's a man or a woman hanging on for dear life over a cliff? Usually when that happens, the person hanging on the cliff is screaming for help. Well that's the battle that we experienced between our flesh and our spirit. For years, our flesh had yearned for the desire or the thrill to live life on the edge, and on our own terms. This force was so deep that we denied our spirit the access into our minds and hearts (our souls). Our spirit fought us for years and protected our flesh from dying or being completely crushed. The flesh enjoyed the dangling of the legs, the work our hands had to put in just to stay in that spot. We stood strong with our flesh and hung on for dear life. Though our spirits (actually the Holy Spirit) was fighting for us—we saw Him and we felt Him, but we would pray and turn away like we were okay hanging onto this cliff. We lived life on the edge in everything we did, EXCEPT business. Our businesses were where we set limits and boundaries. Why was that, you ask? Well it's simple, we had to create an illusion to keep the world away from that scene in our movie, "The Cliff." When it came to business, we put on our mask and went HARD. There was no question or doubt about it. This was the only time we really sought counsel and honored it. How could our business flourish with such flawed flesh? God never leaves us, no matter what. However, when it came to our personal lives we gave the BARE MINIMUM to stay in line with God. There was no regard for what God could really do, because our flesh was being administered by the enemy and it felt good, but only to the flesh, because deep down we were depressed and dying slowly. We could hear the spirit so strong that we would question God. Saying things like, "God, why are you in my business right now?" How dare you question us, God, when we are doing so wrong?" That just shows you that we weren't ready to put in the work. And "Faith without works is dead." Welcome to our mental rollercoaster.

Before I formed you in the womb I knew you;
Before you were born I sanctified you;
I ordained you a prophet to the nations.
Jeremiah 1:5

1. Natasha, 1998

I am so confused. Oh my GOD! I need you. I can't believe this. She overheard me. She heard me talking about how sick that I was, and she found out. I can't believe this. I was in the shower, and she started banging *erratically* on the door, demanding that I come out! Yelling that I couldn't live in her house with a baby. She said that there was no way that I was having a baby, and she would *kill me* if I decided to keep it. She yelled, screamed, and cursed at me. I cannot believe I am going through this. How did I get pregnant? Okay, I know how, but *WHY ME?* At first, when I found out, I thought that there was no possible way that I could have a baby. I am about to be a senior. I am a cheerleader. I have to go to college, and I won't be able to do that or get a cheerleading scholarship. And most importantly, I won't be able to move away from here. OMG, but now all that seems ridiculous. I just don't want to go through this. I can't. Stop her, please! I cannot believe that she is making me have an abortion. If I don't do it, everything will be taken away from me. No place to live, no money, no car, no college. But OMG. This is going to hurt so bad… Okay we're getting closer, God, please stop this car. Stop the world. Stop this woman! Okay let me die. Yes, that's it. Make something happen so that I can die before I have to go in this place. Okay YUCK! This place looks GROSS! It is so dirty here. Police are everywhere. There's a crackhead and drunk guy stumbling around like he's lost his damn mind. It's like eight in the morning. This is crazy. I can't go through this. Are you kidding me???? OMG OMG.

The car stopped.

10

She got out.

She's looking at me.

I'm grabbing my things. This is the last moment that I have with my baby. I have to do something. I'll never meet my baby. What if… What if he or she is supposed to be something great? Okay God, please, if this baby is supposed to live, give me the courage to run.

Judge not, and you will not be judged; condemn not, and you will not be condemned; forgive, and you will be forgiven;
Luke 6:37

2. Sherrell, 2003

Father God in the name of Jesus,

Please forgive me for what I just did. I can't believe I just killed my unborn child. I never thought in a million years that I would kill a baby that would probably mean so much to me. God, I know it was wrong, but neither of us were ready. Is it so bad that I made this decision? What else was I supposed to do? If my father found out he would have went ballistic. If his mother found out she should would be disappointed, and we would never hear the end of it. I was so sick, but now I feel so empty. I feel like a murderer. I love this man so much and I know we would have a pretty baby, but the sickness and the responsibility would be insane right now. Especially since deep down I really want to model. I would never tell DJ, because he would lose his mind. He doesn't believe that his girl is supposed to model. Those are my dreams that he always makes me put to bed, but I'll save that for another prayer on another day. I just need to know what I need to do to get rid of this haunting emotional pain. I need you right now. Help me to escape the screaming taunts from the enemy saying, "You're a horrible person." Lord I know this can't possibly be you, because you are not a God to make me feel like I'm nothing. God, you promised that you would never leave me, and right now I need you to give me a sign telling me that you forgive my actions. Though I know they weren't the best, but I did what I thought was best for me. Is that so wrong? I try not to run from confiding in you before I make any unruly decision only because I JUST know it's wrong. My heart and my spirit tell me to give you a chance wholeheartedly, but then my flesh allows the enemy to take over. The only thing I ask is that you NEVER leave me. Follow me and keep giving me the reason as to why I need to be with you. I know you are asking yourself, who do I think I am giving you orders? You're right. I have NO right to do that with you, God. Deep down I want to know and worship you not only when I need you, but when life is NOT filled with chaos. God, I want to get to the point where I feel like you are deserving of praise every second of every day. I am eighteen and I don't want to live my life regretting the decisions that I have made. I just need you to please forgive me so that I know that my actions are not forgotten, but you have forgiven me.

What will happen with DJ and me?

Will things still be the same?

Will he change?

Are we still going to operate as normal?

Did he REALLY want to keep the baby, but couldn't stand to see me so sick? Those are all of the questions that I will probably go to my grave with besides asking you. Well God, that's it for now. My head is spinning and the light from the sun is piercing through my window and it's making me feel even emptier. Is this depression? SMH. Oh well, I love you God. Amen.

Flee from sexual immorality. Every other sin a person commits is outside the body, but the sexually immoral person sins against his own body.
1 Corinthians 6:18

3. Natasha, 2005

I must confess. In the movies, the people go to the Catholic Church and they can open up a little window, and in the dark, talk to a priest. I know I'm not Catholic, and there's no way I could ever truly "confess" my sins aloud to anyone, so I will confess them directly to you. This pen and pad are my confessional. Lord I know you know these things, but maybe if I write them out, I can rationalize, or you can speak to me and show me what is wrong with me and why I keep doing reckless things in chase of a thrill. I. Feel. So. Disgusting. Help me, please.

Today, the craziest thing happened. I recently bought this house, and I've been feeling lonely, although we are supposedly in a committed relationship. I believe that I was the only one who wanted this house or to move here. Perhaps I rushed it a bit, because I recently got my real estate license. I felt like I was perpetrating by not having a house, while selling houses to other people. *Would people want to buy a house from someone who was just renting an apartment?* Anyway, since we moved, there has been a lot of tension. We have both been consumed with work. I have been traveling back and forth from PG County to Baltimore, working at the newspaper and in the real estate office. So we haven't been spending a lot of time together. We don't have sex, and I feel like "just a friend" most of the time, even though we are supposed to be a couple. I don't feel sexy, and I don't feel attractive. Anyhow, as I was laying on the bed daydreaming today, there was this knock on the door. I looked out of my bedroom window to see the Comcast cable truck outside. Then I leaned over to see the cable guy standing there. He was a young dude, my age. I hurried to straighten up my bed, clean the bathroom, and apply lipstick. Then I ran downstairs and opened the door.

I stared at him as he confirmed he was at the right house. He was there to hookup two cable boxes. I told him he could start downstairs. As he was connecting the wires and going from inside of the house to outside, I sat on the couch, and watched him move. He wasn't fine or anything and he actually needed a haircut, but he had this mysterious appeal. At first, I couldn't quite put my finger on why he seemed so familiar to me. Initially he reminded me of Cee, this dude who I went out with my freshman year and embarrassed me on the yard in front of Cummings Hall and lied. He told all the guys in his dorm that he slept with me. I started rolling my eyes at this cable guy, just thinking about how disgusted Cee made me. I tried to get him expelled from school for harassing me like that. I didn't have a problem admitting who I slept with, but I didn't sleep with him.

He tried it though, and when I said "no" he tried to rip my clothes off, and I ran out of his apartment. I kept staring at the cable guy, trying to figure out if I knew him. I didn't know too many Baltimore dudes… then it hit me! He reminded me of this fine, dark skinned dude from back in the day, John. My mind went south as I remembered the first (and only time) I had sex with John on that crazy New Year's night, when I was still in school. I sat on the couch daydreaming about John, and I remembered how I tugged at his braids as I enjoyed every bit of him. I was right in the middle of a steamy memory when the cable guy's voice snapped me back into reality.

"I'm done. Can you sign here?" he said.

Slowly, I got up from the couch and looked him up and down. He was holding out a pen. We locked eyes and I told him, thank you. And I signed the papers. He tore off the yellow copy and handed it to me, and began to pack up. This was my moment. *Lord, what is it about me that is attracted to the thrill? Why did I have to say anything?*

I asked, "Do you have more houses to go to?"

As if he could read my mind, he said, "I make my own schedule."

"Why don't you come upstairs," I told him.

"You serious?"

"Yeah."

God, I guess I'm confessing this to see if you'll forgive me of yet another horrible thing that I did. My body is so weak.

Natasha, 2006

One of my coworkers has a son, who is a sweetheart. He has this amazing smile, and he works out. He was a football player in high school and college, and he recently started working in the call center at our job. For a week or so, we would randomly bump into each other near the elevators at work. (Side-note: I am also seeing one of the managers in the credit department. He lives nearby and we often leave work to go to his apartment, which is a hot mess. It turns me off, and I think he's dirty, but something overtakes me, because he is so skilled where it counts. He keeps trying to "bring me back to the other side." He's become my lunch break, SMH.)

So back to the coworker's son. I finally went out with him. Then, I invited him over, and… now he is clinging to me. He likes me too much. He just got out of a serious relationship. I still am in a serious, live-in relationship. I feel horrible now. Crazy thing, I have not felt so bad about cheating until I met him. I guess I don't feel bad because I know I don't care about any of these dudes, and I do care about her. But she and I have been together for so long, and it's not really a physical connection that we share. It's a friendship. It's mental. I don't feel bad about dealing with guys, because, God, I feel that you did not create me to be with a woman forever. I know this is only a phase. But I don't want to hurt her. I love her dearly.

Not only do a feel horrible about cheating, but I feel even worse that the coworker's son is really feeling me. His mom thinks I'm such a sweetheart and that I'd be a great match for her son. But now, he wants to bring me home to meet his dad. I think he feels like this is getting serious. I think my sweet, always smiling, demeanor has him confused. I am a nice person. I am a bubbly person. I am a flirtatious person. I think this has misled him. I have to somehow create distance between him and me. I have to cut it off with my other coworker too. Someone is going to get hurt, and unfortunately my heart is so ice cold, and that someone will *not* be me. I feel so heartless. I'm not sure why I do these things. My coworker's son is the first guy who has caught feelings for me in a long time, since my freshman year of college.

Lord, can you show me a way out of this mess, please? I don't want to hurt anyone. Maybe, you should just let me be the one who is heartbroken and hurt this time. Maybe if I get caught, I'll never do this again. God, I'm terrible. I know I keep asking you to forgive me, but I keep living this double life. How will I ever stop?

Create in me a clean heart, O God, and renew a right spirit within me.
Psalm 51:10

4. Sherrell, 2006

Let's NOT talk about sex anymore.

I can't believe that DJ and I are no longer in a relationship. It hurts like hell. However, my cousin gave me a CD with an artist by the name of Tweet. She said it would help and she was right. I have played this album over and over again. I promise if I ever meet her, I am going to tell her the hell my heart has been through and hug her for being so transparent on this album. I may pass out, but at least give me the chance to meet her.

God. I just feel so promiscuous when I am not in a relationship. I need you now more than ever. My flesh is so weak and most times I can't control it. When I see a man that looks even remotely sexy, I immediately think about how he would feel inside of me. I don't want this feeling anymore. However, I love the way men make me feel and then when I am done with them physically, I want no parts of them. It's like I am a Man-eater and I enjoy it while it's happening. Lord, please deliver me from me. I just want to feel normal and not feel the desire to have sex with any and every man that I encounter who I find attractive. God, please protect my flesh.

Last night I went with Rinauda and she introduced me to a guy she knows, and God I know you know and saw what I did. The moment I laid my eyes on that man, I knew immediately that I would have sex with him. God, I know I promised to stop having sex with any man that I found attractive and, at that time, I meant it. That was until I walked in this man's house and saw he had Remy 1738 and weed. The devil played a huge part in me not having anything to do with you, Lord. I'm so sorry that I keep making broken promises to you God. I know you are tired of me apologizing. I will continue to talk to you no matter how bad my situation is. I just want to get to the point where I no longer have to deal with my tainted flesh. It's so destroyed. How could I have locked myself in a room with a man I just met and have sex with him for over six hours? All the while my best friend is on the other side of the door banging on it trying to figure out what I could possibly be doing for six hours, in a room with a man I just met. God, hear my soul crying out. Snatch me out of my pit of sexual addiction. I am not good for anyone in the state I am in. God, help heal me, so I can evolve into the woman you need me to be. My mind is not made up, but I know what I am doing is wrong and destructive and I want to stop but this temptation of doing something so wrong and it feeling so right and so exhilarating, and I truly enjoy the thrill. My spirit is just so sick of me falling deeper and deeper into the pit of self-destruction. SAVE ME GOD. You promised that you will never leave nor forsake me, well where are you? Where are you when I let those men on top of me and me on top of them? Where were you? Can you even hear me? It doesn't matter Granny told me you were real, so I'll continue to pray and have an ounce of faith that one day you will hear me and help save me.

Amen.

Sherrell, June 2007

God, my life is like a whirlwind. I jumped out of one relationship and now I find myself in another whole relationship that is so toxic for me. This man has introduced me to everyone I need to be connected with in order to make my way in the industry. He knows everyone, but God I know he is a snake. How could I love a snake? How could I let a snake lay on top of me or me on top of him and let him experience my flesh so deeply like this? I just want to get out of this relationship. But I am scared, because he will try to ruin me if I leave him. People may not want to work with me if I am no longer with him. I need him right? God, please answer me. Show me what to do. Is it that I am drinking and smoking and blocking my blessings? I promise that I will give it up. Slow walk me, God. Every sign in the world is telling me to leave. Please give me another sign...

I know I asked you to give me a sign, but did I have to go through pain and trauma in order to receive the sign? I cannot believe I was almost raped on the train in broad daylight. To make matters worse, he thought I was making it up. Not only did he think I was lying, but he was out with that young girl all day, and now he's in the club with her, freaking all on her.

- God, to make matters really worse, it's 4 a.m. and he's is still not home.

- Lord, I really don't want to get in this car to go to this girl's house. Please stop me. Never mind. It's going down.

- Lord Jesus, I am so mad, and I am running all these stop signs and red lights. God, just get me there. I know you don't answer these type of prayers, so I will just ask that you stay with me while I go handle this trifling dude.

-Lord, when I pull up to this girl's house, I pray to you and everyone in heaven that this man is not here.

-Omgoodness his car is here, and it's in the cut. God, is he crazy?? Oh no, it's going down. Good thing Bossy and G wanted to come. This may get ugly.

-God, you still there? I am about to run up in this girl's house. I know I am working for the enemy, but please cover me while I'm doing it. I know I am making some wild requests, but my flesh is weak to that spirit, and all I know how to do is feed it and talk to you while I do it. Does this make me insane? Either way I had to handle this. He's in there with a minor, cheating on me AGAIN. God, I have had two abortions and one miscarriage with this man. He doesn't deserve me anymore. As I look down at my left ring finger and see this engagement ring, it hits me that it's only a "hush ring." This man can't possibly want to marry me. He doesn't show it at all.

I am done God. I am going to finish vandalizing his car and busting his teeth out his mouth, and then I will go home and throw all of his belongings out in the street. I'M DONE!

Amen.

⌒

Sherrell, 2008

Father God in the name of Jesus,

I know my prayers are becoming so redundant. I am sorry for being so weak and working for the enemy most of the time. God, it's just easier. Have I been called to work directly for you? If so, I have to decline. I don't think I have the qualifications to work for you. I pray to you and ask for forgiveness, but it's like I slip right back into my sin. That is why I know that

GOD MADE ME WAIT!

I am not the one for whatever this job is you are trying to appoint me to. I know I promised that I wouldn't get another abortion, but God I know you know and saw that this man is STILL not the one for me. God, why am I here? I know you can't possibly have me here to rejoice in your name, or do you? He is cheating on me daily, getting me pregnant, and wanting me to get rid of "it" as soon as we find out that I am pregnant. This relationship with this man is just not going to work. I continuously have sex with him and let him do his business and now I'm the one stuck with an unborn baby. He has stolen from me. Oh God, please let me just vent for a second.

Last month, I came home to see my window broken out and the only thing that was stolen was my laptop. God something doesn't seem right. Why was my laptop the only thing missing? The broken window where the supposed robber "broke in" was so small. God it was no way possible that even the smallest crackhead could get in. I am starting to think he faked this whole robbery to pay a debt back with my laptop. God show me. Reveal his actions to me so I can have all the more reason to leave him...

Really, God? I ask you to give me a sign, and I have to receive it like this? Did he really do exactly what I thought he did?!? Is that my laptop on his "business partner's" desk? I couldn't push myself to be bold enough to ask him aloud. Not because I was scared of him telling me the truth. I was more so afraid of him lying and then me faking like I believe him or just settling for the lie yet AGAIN. God, SNATCH me away from him. Obviously, I can't escape this man by myself any longer. SNATCH ME, SNATCH ME, PLEASE SNATCH ME!!!!

God, please rescue me and save me from my own self destruction. I don't want to be used and looked at as an object anymore. Please help me to escape the need to be loved by these men. I just can't escape my flesh. It yearns for more attention than my spirit. I ignore my spirit until I have nothing else to give. God, he cheats on me every chance he gets. I try to ignore some incidents, and then some I address. How can I possibly think it's okay to have sex with this man? God, he can't love me like he says he does, because I wouldn't feel so empty and alone. Will a man who loves you make you feel like you have to prove yourself? God, please help me to understand. God, I promised you years ago that I would never do this again, and here I am three abortions later, and I AM DONE! Save me from this relationship and this desire to not be alone. I promise this is it!
Amen.

Do not give what is holy to the dogs; nor cast your pearls before swine, lest they trample them under their feet, and turn and tear you in pieces.

Matthew 7:6

5. Natasha, 2009

Hey, so there's this saying, that "if it seems too good to be true, it probably is." Well, I don't think that's in your word Lord, so it's not necessarily true right? Maybe I just want to believe that this "good thing" is true.

I met this guy JD last night. It was a blind date. I was in Baltimore, for a conference and my sister's friend, who is dating his best friend, set it up. We talked once over the week, but then, I met him in person. At first I was pissed. He was late. I was staying in the Marriott on the Harbor, and he was supposed to be there around 7. He didn't get there until 10 (STRIKE ONE), and I was at the hotel bar. He came up, and he was so sexy. *Lord, why did he have to look so sexy? I was hoping that he was ugly in person so I wouldn't feel bad about carrying him.* I could tell off the top that he had money, and he looked like a dope boy. And it's not like I'm a money-hungry chick or nothing. I have my own, but it's good to have a guy who *looks* the part. "You like what you see?" I said to him, and he replied, "I love it, baby." We had a couple of drinks, then ate seafood. We walked around the Harbor, and stopped in ESPN Zone. I told him all about the new communications company I am starting, and he said he wanted me to meet his friend, who is a promoter for all the rap shows in DC. I am in Pennsylvania, and I need all the connects in DC that I can get, so that I can kill it when I move back home. After we walked around the harbor, talking for a while, I invited him back up to my room. That was a mistake.

Okay God, I know you already know what I did, but maybe I can just tell you why. I think that he's special. He likes me and he's exactly what

I've been missing. I can't believe I had sex with him. I told myself I wasn't going to, but I got drunk, and I wanted to. We had an amazing time, and it was *sooo good.* The next morning, I didn't want him to leave. He didn't want to leave either. It's like we were made to stay right there in that moment forever. *Please let him be THE ONE.* Thank you.
Amen.

*N*atasha, 2009

Okay God, I finally realize my problem. I have an addiction – to sex, to men, and to control. It's an addiction to the control I have during sex. I looked it up, and addiction is a persistent, compulsive dependence on a behavior or substance. I *persistently, compulsively* depend on this high I get from the thrill of SEX! I like controlling them with my body, and I like being controlled. And now I have met a man, JD, who is my match. He's addicted to sex and women, and I can't stand it. Well, the sex thing is fine, but not the women. I want him to be addicted to me and only me, and I'm determined to make that happen. I crave him, and he's treating me like anything. I know that he sleeps with other women when I'm in PA during the week, and so it makes me want to quit my job and move home ASAP. *I'm so weak for him. SMH.*

Anyway, he has been trippin' lately. Granted, I know I acted a little crazy the last time he saw me. Me and my homegirl Ken met him at Love the Club. He didn't know we were coming, but when he saw my face and locked eyes with me, he smiled and gestured for me to come into the VIP section. The first thing he told me, was, "Do not get drunk. Do not embarrass me." That night his fam, a former NBA player, was having a birthday celebration. At first everything was all good. We were on the stage, and the guys were poppin' bottles and pouring champagne. Then I started dancing with these two girls and we were kissing on stage, and I started drinking glass after glass of champagne. After that, it happened. I slipped and fell and his cousin – the basketball player – told security to come and get me. I was so embarrassed. I have NEVER BEEN KICKED OUT OF A CLUB BEFORE!! He has been tripping since that night, and, he's acting differently. I think I messed up. So my mind is shifting. I gotta move on, right? I feel so rejected. *Maybe this is you actually releasing me from this addictive situation. I can't stop thinking about him. Why does sex make me so attached? Why did I have sex with him so soon?*

I had been looking at my phone all day, hoping that JD would call. I came in town this morning, and he knows that I'm here, and he hasn't hit me up yet. I go back to PA tomorrow, and I really want to see him bad. I know that if we do it, he'll think twice about letting me go. I know he cannot resist me. It just so happened that John, a "friend," who I met in ATL years ago hit me up tonight. Oh boy…The funny thing about John is that we don't even like each other. We simply use each other. Year after year, maybe just a few times a year… It MUST BE THE THRILL! It all started that night in Atlanta, in 2000/2001, when my team went to cheer at a big HBCU football tournament. My teammates and I decided to go to the club, and OF COURSE I got drunk. The entire night is a blur, and the only memories that I can recall are pushing the tables together in the club, then standing on top of them, dancing. I saw this dude in the dark. He stood out, from all of the guys. Maybe it was his height, or his hair. OMG, his hair was like that! He had long cornrows, and his hair was silky. His skin was chocolate. He was tall, maybe 6'2 or 6'3, and he was bowlegged. I immediately gestured to him with my head, and told him to come to me. I hopped off the table, and slid through the crowd of people, and over to meet him. He was smiling, and he asked my name. I told him. He was so fine. OMG. I found out that he was a sophomore like me, and he attended school in NC. But he was from back home. From that moment, I knew that we'd be *very good friends.*

We kept in touch over the next several months. In February, me and some of my teammates *just had to go to NBA All Star Weekend.* It was in DC, and since we were just 45 minutes away at Morgan, it would've been blasphemy if we didn't go. So we hopped in the car at like one in the morning. It was so spur-of-the moment. We were walking out of DC Live, after a couple hours of partying, and guess who I spotted at the door? You would not believe it, but it was HIM. My fine, sexy chocolate, bow-legged friend. OMG. I went up to him, stood in front of him, and I said, *"What's up, baby?"* HA! He smiled and said, *"What's up, Tash?"* I nodded, and from that day it was on. He was so fine. I wanted him that moment!

We finally slept together on New Year's Day the following year. It was about two or so in the morning. We both had a really chill New Year's Eve, and he hit me up. I wasn't at my apartment in Baltimore, but I would be for him. I told him to be at my apartment in an hour. It was on.

This crazy lust has been going on for eight years now. *What's wrong with me? I'm a business owner and a professional. People look up to me! They think I'm "a good girl."* And he's no better! He has a family (with his girlfriend), children, and a six-figure salary. He works overnight, and I am rarely in the DMV, but when I am, he hits me up. We communicate over

Google chat. He pops up on my screen at random hours of the night, usually around 2 or 3 a.m. We don't text or call each other. All he ever says is, "What up? You home?" Even when I'm not home, I say yes. Because I *will be soon for him.* We have sex in his truck most of the time. There's been a lot of back seat rendezvous. I feel like a slut whenever I'm with him, even though I'm not sleeping with a lot of people. I am so ashamed. I have to be so "good" all the other time and uphold this image that everyone thinks of me. But they don't realize that I have an addiction, an urge. And I am sleeping with someone that *I'll never be in a relationship with.* It's not that I want to be in a relationship with him. Our hookups are always in the middle of the night before he goes home to his girl and his children. Although he's not married, and I know he's not happy, I know it's wrong. I don't even like him. In fact, I can't stand him. We recently tried to link up during the day, and we tried to have an actual conversation, because maybe we both felt a little awkward only being wanted for one reason, but the conversation didn't work.

After thirty seconds, I started to get turned off.

We started arguing.

I can't stand his personality.

I told him to shut up.

All I want is sex.

All I want is to feel him inside of me. And I feel bad, because I'm starting to want that feeling more and more. Now that JD is acting stupid, I must get someone to fill his role, and John isn't a new guy. He wouldn't be a new body, so it only seems right to hit him up. I am beginning to crave the control I feel whenever we link up and he comes over. I've begun to time it just right. He gets off from work at 4:45 a.m. He gets out of his controlled building around 4:55. I hit him up on Google (or he contacts me) around 5:10, and by that time, he's crossed the bridge, and he's on Indian Head Highway. I tell him I want to see him. He is at my house in eight minutes. I come outside. He turns off his headlights, pulls a condom out of his glove compartment. I climb in the backseat. He gets on top of me... And then, I'm taken away by the pain, the pleasure.

I need a release FROM ME. *Can you help me?* I lust him. I fiend for JD. They're both like drugs. This life that has me feeling so dirty and ashamed is becoming a dangerous habit. Nothing can stay in the dark forever. *I'm so sorry, God. I'm a horrible person. I am not worthy of anything that I have... not this house, this career, this business, these clients. I wouldn't blame you if you took it all away just to make me pay for what I've done.*

> *For the Lord sees not as man sees: man looks on the outward appearance, but the Lord looks on the heart.*
> **1 Samuel 16:7**

6. Sherrell, 2009

I can't believe I have to have this conversation with my parents. God, how did I end up sleeping from hotel to hotel? I am SO SICK of acting like I have it all together for the public all because I have created this illusion of Sherrella La Bella and now I have to live up to it EVERY DAY. I just want to be normal again, and stop faking like I have this and that when my life is really in shambles. God, why am I even putting myself through this? I don't have to live like this. I *just had to* move out of my parent's house and be on my own. Now since I am out here, I feel like I have to do whatever to survive. God, this is not my life. This is not who I am. Why am I pretending that I have to survive in this manner? Help me to get out of this slump. God, am I depressed and hiding it? SMH. I just wish I had the answers to why I self-destruct every chance I get. The public has no clue that I am a hot ass damn mess. I'm sorry for cursing God, but I am TIRED. Where did I go wrong with my life? Am I really about to ask my parents to stay with them? I can't go back. My money is running low, and I don't have money to throw away *just* to keep staying in hotels.

I couldn't push myself to ask my parents to stay with them. However, what I did do was far worse. That man meant nothing to me. I hate that I did what I did. That was so traumatizing… God, he didn't deserve me. He has been chasing me for years, and I finally decide to give him a

chance....UUUUGGGGH! But why did I have to do it under those circumstances? I never want to see him again. I am a damn mess, and I am sick
of it. God, I just want to escape this bad habit. I want to escape me. Who have
I become? I wasn't raised this way. Why do I live a life that causes so much
pain? Who do I owe? Who do I owe my life God? You and only you, right?
Then why do I continuously serve the enemy? I want OUT!!!! I have major
events coming up that I paint with glitter and gold, and behind-the-scenes the
events of my personal life are a mess painted with darkness and not a single
ounce of light. UGGGGH I WANT OUT. God, please continue to stay with
me. I am a mess and I am sick of it. I need help from you. Taunting scenes
of what I have done haunt me, and I try to drink it away in the clubs and sex
it away with men that couldn't care less about me. I WANT OUT! GOD, I
NEED YOU TO STAY WITH ME. I love you for staying with me all this
time and never leaving or judging me. I will get better. I will serve you
wholeheartedly one day. I promise.
Amen.

***In your anger do not sin:" Do not let the sun go down while
you are still angry, and do not give the devil a foothold.***
Ephesians 4:26-27

7. Natasha, 2009

God, can you please help my temper? I have a problem with being disrespected. I have a problem with females who come at me like I won't smack them, and I especially have a problem with these bougie club chicks in DC that think they're better than everyone! I don't fit in. This week, I'm celebrating my birthday, and I had been feeling down about things being over with JD. Of course my little sister wanted to make my weekend amazing, so Friday night, we went out to The Park nightclub, and it was nuts. This girl thought she was cute, because she and her friends were in VIP, and we weren't. I guess she felt some type of way, because the guys at her table were making room for us. Anyway, she came out of her mouth at me wrong, and I tried to pimp slap her in the middle of the club. This promoter, Dre, who I have been doing PR for over the last couple of months was there, and he scooped me up and broke up the ensuing fight just as the security guards were coming to kick us out. That was Friday night.

Lord Jesus, please help my temper. I have absolutely no chill. I feel like my bottled up anger is going to get me in big trouble one day. I felt so terrible afterwards, and extremely embarrassed that my client was there. I have to be a boss at all times if I'm going to be a successful publicist. I may not ever step foot in The Park again! God, please make it so this incident does not follow me. I'm so glad people don't really know me yet. Thank you for hiding me, I am obviously not ready to be a "public figure."

*N*atasha, 2009

My birthday weekend actually ended up being a turning point in my life, and now I'm deep into a life that may be a bit dangerous. Just when I was starting to fall into a deep depression, thinking about JD, he became a non-issue. After my family got in a huge argument and embarrassed me at my b-day dinner at The Chart House, all I wanted to do was smoke and drink. We didn't have any weed, so I randomly stopped at the gas station, and bought my first pack of cigarettes and proceeded to chain smoke them. Then my sister, her friend, and I headed to Layla Lounge, where they have a really chill Monday night event.

Out of nowhere, I met this guy. I was standing outside smoking a cigarette, and he heard me telling the manager that it was my birthday. He told me that I shouldn't be smoking and suggested that I put out the cigarette and meet him at the bar so he could buy me some bottles. Well, at first, I was so irritated and annoyed that he had commented on my cigarette, and I was so busy sulking in self-pity, missing JD, upset and heartbroken that my birthday dinner had been ruined, and desperately wanting this new year of life to bring better situations. In the past year, I had left a relationship, rented out the house in Baltimore, moved out of the house that I shared with my girl in PA into a tiny, little apartment two minutes away her, mentally checked-out of my job, started a business, fell for a "player," and got my heartbroken. I run back and forth from DC to PA every weekend, and now there I was on my birthday unsure of what the future would hold. The club manager's voice made me wake up.

"My man ain't faking. You should go inside and meet him at the bar." I threw down the cigarette and asked, "Did he say he wanted to buy me drinks or bottles?"

"Bottles. That man definitely said bottles," the guys outside assured me, as if dude was ballin' like that. *Whatever,* I thought.

I walked in and introduced myself to my new friend. I'll call him Ant. He was ordering a bottle of vodka and a bottle of rosé. We toasted and introduced ourselves. After a few drinks, he asked me if I wanted to look at videos in his truck. He drove a black Range, and we sat inside of it watching music videos and talking for the next couple of hours. When my sister and her friend started blowing up my phone, I went inside and got them, so that we could go home.

So here's where I am so confused. I know that my life has just up-graded. I am quickly becoming addicted to this new lifestyle. He's so sweet and he'll do anything for me, but I sense, after a few days that he is involved in something illegal. He told me to never ever go through his phone, because he wants to keep me completely out of that life. I promised him that I would-n't. But I think he figures I'm innocent and I know nothing about "that life." LOL. If he only knew...

I've been at his house non-stop for the past few months. He has me driving his cars. He takes me shopping, and his place is like my own personal getaway. When I come home from PA on the weekends, sometimes, he and I stay in nice hotel rooms on the National Harbor, or we go out of town to remote spots, and if we can't do that, he gives me a ton of money and tells me to do what I want. One weekend, he had me call all my friends and my sister over to his house, and he paid for a masseuse to come over and pamper us. He went out with his homies and me and my girls enjoyed massages and rosé at his place. It's definitely a life I could get used to...

The other day, when Ant came home, I was arguing on the phone with one of my clients. I was PISSED, because he owed me $200. I was screaming to the top of my lungs at him, calling him out on all of his BULL when my babe walked in and grabbed the phone out of my hand. Ant hung up the phone in the middle of my yelling and slammed it on the table.

"Don't ever let me hear you pressing another nigga out over $200," he said. Then he slammed some fifties on the table. "There's $200. He does-n't owe you anything."

After that, he said something to me that no one has ever said. I immediately realized how valuable I was.

"You are the best publicist in DC. You are Natasha Brown. You are the baddest bitch in the city. You don't need a nigga for nothing. They need you. You are brilliant. You hear me? You are a boss. From now on, you will not drive your car to any of your meetings or events. You will drive one of mine. Everyone needs to know that you are that BAD. They need to know that you're a boss. Do you hear me?"

I was honestly in shock. By this time, my emotions were out of control after the argument I had just had. It was the sweetest thing that I have heard, even despite the "bitch." I shook my head and said okay. Then he went in his bathroom and ran the water, poured bubble bath in the tub, lit some candles, and told me to go relax, while he sat on the couch and watched the game.

God, I am happy to have him in my life, and I know that he cares about me. However, there is something that I cannot quite put my finger on yet. God, can you please reveal it to me? What am I missing here?

And I know it is important to love him with all my heart and all my understanding and all my strength, and to love my neighbor as myself. This is more important than to offer all of the burnt offerings and sacrifices required in the law.
Mark 12:33

8. Sherrell, 2009

God,

I don't know where this feeling came from, but for some reason I feel so powerful like I can take over the world now that AP and I are done. I feel like a free bird. Being in that relationship, I relinquished so much control over my life, and I was subconsciously unaware. God, I guess I was just in it for the thrill of living on the edge. I now question my actions and the sacrifices I made with him. Like for example, what made you stay with me Lord when I decided to sleep on the floor of an empty studio building? God, you know I didn't have to do that. My parents would have happily taken me in. Why did I sleep in my car many nights just to show him that I was his ride or die? I didn't have to put myself in that mess, but I did all in the name of "love."

God, if that is what love is I don't want to experience that ever again. When I think about how I sacrificed my physical appearance and my safety by sleeping in these random places, because we had no money and "no place to go," it scares me that I could be so easily manipulated to believe that my life was something that it really doesn't have to be. God, I knew deep down that wasn't the type of lifestyle for me. I just wanted to prove to my family that I was doing "okay" and to prove to AP that no other woman was a better fit for him than me. SMH. Oh God, how INSANE does all this sound? Where did I develop such an insecurity? How do I get rid of it? And also is it gone since I removed myself from him? I pray to you every day about my life, and yet I still make these irrational decisions. God, I pray that I can have the same spiritual confidence as I do when I do business. I pray that my flawed heart and mind are taken over by you. Do I submit all of me in order to receive you? Omgoodness and what does that look like? I am afraid of transitioning from me now to that me. What will people think? I know most would think I am a hypocrite. God, I am just not fully ready to submit all of me to you, but PLEASE DON'T LEAVE ME. I know this sounds crazy, but can you pray for me?

I think things are going to be different now that my sister and my niece are staying with me. She helps balance me out. Not to mention she has stopped me from countless rendezvous with men. God, did you send her here to give me a sign? She talks to me every night about my behavior. She was shocked about the way I have been carrying myself. Normally, I would defend myself, but this is my sister and she knows me more than anybody, so I just let all walls down and confide in her as I do you. God, can she see the hurt and the mask I put on? Does she know I yearn for something that I may never find if I don't submit to you? Well for whatever reason she is here, I accept. I want to change and I need your help, so I will try my hardest to change. Unfortunately, this power that I feel is a little intense because it feels like I have to seek revenge, prove a point, and WIN. But when I say WIN, God, I don't mean for you. It is more of a vindictive win. SMH. Please save me from my own self-destruction.

I am so excited that I started Honeycomb Set. I have gotten calls from so many promoters from the top clubs in DC. They want MY models to promote and come to their events. The moment I started to promote the models, the calls and emails began to come in and fast. Honeycomb Set is getting bigger and bigger each week. We are taking over so many clubs, and everyone knows who we are. I make sure to be aggressive and only show that I am a BOSS. So to make matters worse, and to prove how serious I am, today I am going to ask my sister to take me to the tattoo parlor to get a tattoo of a honeycomb on my neck. I know she is going to think I am crazy for this. When I hear my thoughts, it's a little hard to believe that this is me. SMH. Has this illusion of Sherrella La Bella completely taken over my life? God, I like this feeling of power, however when I replay conversations or even my thoughts in my head, it is a little hard to listen to. Ohhhh God, just please continue to stay with me.
Amen.

No one can serve two masters, for either he will hate the one and love the other, or he will be devoted to the one and despise the other. You cannot serve God and money.
Matthew 6:24

9. Natasha, Thanksgiving, 2009

I was drunk and high, and I couldn't sleep. I thought about hitting up this girl I had recently met, Sherrella, because she is always out and up to something. I needed to take my mind off of things. I had this bubbling anxiety that I just couldn't place. Ant went to sleep early, and I was bored. We have matching phones. I was on the couch, playing a game on my phone. I put it down, and picked his up instead of mine once I was ready to play it again. I started typing on the phone, and I noticed missed text messages. By this time, I knew that I had picked up his phone, but I couldn't put it down. It was attached to my hand as if Superglue had bonded us. I went to the text messages. They were from someone labeled "Her." I opened the first text and saw these pictures of this whack chick in a Halloween costume that looked like an exotic bunny rabbit. I then scrolled back and saw more messages. And more. They were talking about hooking up. She wanted to come over for Thanksgiving, and he gave her an excuse. He told her that she was good the last time he felt her. Immediately my blood started boiling, and I think I thought that I was screaming inside, but then I heard my voice. I screamed and yelled so loud. I don't think I said anything specific, it was just a loud UGHHHHAAAAHHHHH. I must have scared the shit out of him, because he jumped up out of his bed so fast, and I heard him stumble across his floor. He appeared in the living room in a matter of seconds.

"What's wrong baby? You okay?"

Seeing the care in his face, I immediately felt guilty, but I had to know what the hell was going on. "WHAT IS THIS?? WHO IS "HER?""

"Huh? What are you talking about?

"Don't huh me? What is this?"

"You didn't. Please don't tell me you went through my phone.
OH HE WAS AWAKE NOW.

"I told you don't ever go through my phone, Natasha. I told you that it would be over the minute you went through my phone."

"Yeah, but you told me you wanted to keep me out of the shit that you do, NOT away from the hoes you're sleeping with. You didn't tell me that I would find half naked girls in your phone. How could you do this to me?"

In his calmest voice, as if he was at peace with this decision AND HE WAS RIGHT, he said that it was over. He told me that he loved me but now he couldn't trust me. "You don't have to leave now, but tomorrow, I want you to pack up your stuff and leave. I want my keys back. I can't be with you anymore, because I can't trust you."

I must admit that this was so G of him, but God why did I begin to apologize? Why did I say that I was sorry, because he said it was over? I started crying, and I started acting a damn fool. *It can't be over* was all I could think. I will not go back to my life as it was. I really hate being rejected. I saw my life, this image that I had built, shatter before my eyes. I could not, would not, accept that it was over. I cried myself to sleep in his bed, and he slept on the couch. The next day, I went out to buy a Black & Mild. He caught me smoking on the balcony and he looked at me with the most disgusting look ever. Neither of us mentioned me leaving all day. I was walking on eggshells, even though HE should have been the one in the doghouse. I was secretly angry and I resented him for playing me like a yo-yo.

"When you met me I was smoking. Why are you acting like that?" I snapped. It was the first thing I had said all day.

He rolled his eyes, and said, "You promised that you'd stop smoking. No girl of mine can be a smoker."

Was this his way of telling me that he wasn't breaking up with me? I was annoyed and pissed. I would make him pay BIG TIME.

Hip-Hop 4 Haiti &The DMV Awards

At the beginning of 2010, Natasha was doing PR for the DMV Music Awards and Sherrell was providing models for the event for the third year in a row. However, our business plans were put on hold on January 12, 2010. There was a devastating earthquake in Haiti. Everything stopped and our focus turned to contributing to relief efforts. We partnered with a national movement called Hip-Hop 4 Haiti, a simultaneous set of relief concerts around the globe in 32 cities. We held two events in DC and sent hundreds of clothes and canned goods to the residents of Haiti. The events we coordinated pulled in many of the top indie rap artists, DJs, and talent in the DMV. We had an amazing time giving back and it was one of the first opportunities we had to learn each other's work ethic.

10. Natasha, 2010

On Christmas of last year, Ant's sons were home, and I tried to play housewife, by cooking everyone a nice meal. But they all laughed at my cooking and refused to eat it. I felt like a rejected people-pleaser who could not please anyone. God, I feel like a trophy. But he plays these mind games. At first, he didn't want me to lift a finger, and when I tried to do anything, he'd insist that I "rest" as if I was some elderly woman. Now, he complains whenever anything is out of place or my work is scattered across the table. He doesn't respect what I do or that I work from home. He bothers me when I'm writing and asks me to do menial chores like put up the dishes or vacuum the floor as soon as I get in my creative flow. WTF. *I'm writing!* He doesn't understand that work is the only thing that makes me happy. To make things worse, he interrupts my flow, and insists that I close my laptop to go out with him to the CLUB or he goes alone, and I'm left wondering if and when he'll make it back safely. I don't even like clubs, but he has to go out. On Wednesdays it's Josephine's. Fridays it's Lux. Saturday nights it's Layla Lounge and Stadium, the strip club, and on Sundays, he goes out with his friends. I HATE going to the clubs with him. It's cool to be in VIP, but I hate that chicks look at me crazy, and I'm forced to keep my cool when I want to smack them. I always want to leave the club and go outside and smoke, but I can't because I am *"Ant's girl."*

Everyone knows me as *Ant's girl.* It sucks because the guys from *Shy Magazine* or *EliteDC Magazine* have caught me on camera chilling with him in the club and one of the magazines posted pics on the Internet. It's really crazy because after the club each night, everyone goes online to get their pics to post on Facebook. The other week, I got cussed out by JD because some hater chick showed him a picture of me sitting on Ant's lap, in Layla Lounge. JD was PISSED! We don't deal with each other anymore, and I found out he's messing with one of my former teammates, but still. We have this sick connection, and I know he's thinking about me. How do I know this? Because, I'm thinking about him. Lord, I hope I am making you laugh right now, because I'm sure laughing at myself and this craziness. I sometimes feel like I can channel JD if I concentrate hard enough. I truly can't explain it. We shared some amazing (and crazy) moments. OMG I just thought about the time after his show with Soulja Boy. We went to the "let out" at Josephine's. He went inside and asked me to sit in the driver's seat. I did, and of course I would have to attract attention. I was looking FINE that night. So this guy comes up to the car and tries to holla at me. JD came out at that exact moment. He said, "I know this nigga ain't tryin' to talk to my girl while she sitting in *my car!*" He was LIVID! But it gave him the perfect opportunity to flex. He reached in the passenger seat, and pulled out a gun and pointed it at the dude and told him to leave. CRAZY right?

Anyway, I know this ain't right God, but I was happy that JD saw that picture I took with Ant and that I got under his skin, but I was also a little blown. I compare the two. Ant treats me better and he's so laid back and established well beyond anything he might be doing in the streets. Meanwhile JD is super amped all the time and ready to turn up in a minute. My personality is more like JD's, but maybe I'll mature a little with Ant. *In this season right now, we belong together and JD or no other dude is comparing to this.* We eat at really nice restaurants. He spoils me, my family and friends, and he shows off in a really humble type of way. He's perfected this baller life, and not only that. You know my theme song is "Boss Lady" by Rick Ross. With Ant, it's definitely "Deeper than Rap"! I gotta keep him around. When I am with him, *everyone* knows I'm the boss's girl. He and I always drive one of his exotic cars. He pulls up to the front of every club, and he knows *everyone.* And I'm his trophy.

Not only am I his trophy, but I know he has a wandering eye. I'm his beautiful trophy, Boss Lady, that he likes to take off the mantel to show off. Everything is all good as long as I keep my mouth shut.

I should have known something was up, God. I believe that you protected me, but I can't believe that this has happened. I had been at Ant's house for a few weeks straight over the holidays and through the New Year. Random people kept knocking on the door. The other day, we rode out to VA where one of the connects live, and we found out dude had been arrested. He immediately panicked. *Okay, let me focus. I need YOU to give me clarity!* Random people have been knocking on his door while he's been at work for the past few weeks. I keep telling them he's not home. At first it was someone wanting to do random maintenance. I told them that the owner wasn't home, and they needed to come back. Then, a Census guy came to the door and asked how many people were living in the house. I told the guy that I couldn't give him any information, and he needed to come back when the owner was home.

It was 5a.m. I was laying in the bed, half naked. I had on panties and one of his oversized t-shirts. Then I heard this loud bang, simultaneously, a bright light came through the hallways, loud voices were yelling something I couldn't quite make out in my sleepy state, and in a matter of seconds, federal agents were standing in front of the bed, with guns blaring in our faces. One of the men in full armor reached on the bed, snatched me up, and threw me into the living room on the floor. Then he put handcuffs on me. They ordered Ant to get on the floor and I could hear the handcuffs rattling and snapping shut. I kept yelling, "Can I put some clothes on, please?" But they didn't care that my ass was in the air. *God, what have I gotten myself into!?* As I sat on the couch handcuffed, about twenty federal agents, and a few with dogs, began trashing his place. I watched as they went through every spot. The candles, which were not really candles, yeah the police picked those up first. They fidgeted for a second and began to screw the first candle apart. I held my breath *and prayed* that they wouldn't find anything there. By this time, Ant was on the couch beside me. I was looking at him. He was SO COOL as they began to tear apart the ottoman. I knew they wouldn't find anything there. I felt like we had bought some time. They were looking in the vents, the shoe boxes. The cops didn't find anything except the candles. They found the car keys and began to question me about which car was mine. One cop began to unscrew the flat screen television. I saw another one take the keys, and I knew he was going outside to search the cars. I wasn't worried, because my nigga was too smart to keep anything in his car. As I was sitting on the couch in my panties and handcuffs, I just kept praying. I kept thinking that he had to quit this game. I couldn't take it anymore. His business had been raided a few weeks ago, and now they had invaded the very place where we lay our heads. After they spent the next hour thoroughly searching the place, they took him out and said they were arresting him. They must've found the evidence they needed.

The entire time, I never panicked. It was weird. I felt like I was bred for this. *A TRUE thoroughbred.* Since I was 15, I dated dope dealers. My first real boyfriend taught me the game. I use to watch his parents cook coke in the kitchen on the same stove as they boiled potpourri. The gas station I worked at became his drugstore. I am not green to this game, but I had never been so close to being caught up as I was on this day. Only by *Your grace,*

God did this pan out the way it did.

Once he was gone, they removed my handcuffs, and told me that they had no evidence that I had been involved. They confiscated his phones and the keys to his cars. They had bags of "evidence" as well. I went into hustle mode. Once they were gone, I called his cousin, and we began to put a plan in motion. I asked myself, *what is he going to need immediately when he gets out? What would he want me to do?* I went and purchased another throwaway phone and called his business partners. Then I went to pick up his cousin, and we began to inform his other partners of what happened. That day, I just prayed. *God, I am convinced that you answer the sinners' prayers.* That night, around 9, I got a call from him. I think he was at the FBI precinct in Baltimore. They were letting him go. I thought it was odd. To be honest, I thought it was *real* odd. I'll leave that right there.

This was such a close call. I found it very suspect that his place was hit too. This game is so shady. I don't trust anyone. I smell a snitch.

But God shows his love for us in that while we were still sinners,
Christ died for us.
Romans 5:8

11. Sherrell, 2009

Hey God,

Things are moving so fast with this event. I have pulled in some heavy hitters, and I have all of the Honeycomb Set models out promoting. We are running into everyone, because we are hitting the "let-outs" at all the hottest parties in the city. The people we are running into will make this event so beneficial. However God, I am getting distracted by this one guy. He was so close to me when AP and I were together. Since I had the studio in my apartment, AP used to have so many people coming in and out during that short time to record music, voice overs, etc. I met so many people including CK. He would come over and cook for all of the models and artists in my place. He would also bring so much weed, and we would just talk for hours. Even though he was really supposed to be there to record music, he rarely did. I honestly think that AP was intimidated by his talent so he never really questioned the closeness of our relationship. I think he liked it because he didn't have to stick his chest out to show who was the better artist. Okay, so fast forward to now, I keep seeing him at the "let-outs." God, is this a sign that I am supposed to pursue an intimate relationship with him? One of my close friends who is also a Honeycomb Set model kept telling me she thinks he likes me before that whole mess popped off with AP and me. God, I don't want to mess our friendship up. What do I do?

I am so sorry, God. I didn't hear you respond to me about CK, so I took matters into my own hands. I cannot believe we have gotten so close and, not only that, we have had sex and cannot go an hour without talking on the phone or seeing each other. I have always liked him as a friend, but now he is becoming almost like a boyfriend. God, this is all happening too fast, but I don't want to stop it. I know I should not be this heavily involved with another man ALREADY. I just need to focus on work. Where have I developed this need to be loved by men? Why do I feel like sex is the answer to everything? My parents have always displayed love in its rarest form. God, where have I gone wrong? Just please stay with me.

Amen.

Airwaves

This year was so insane. In addition to everything happening in our personal lives, 2010 was the year that EliteDC radio launched. Sherrell had a show called "On the Leather With Sherrella." It was a late-night sex talk show that was extremely LIT! There were several cohosts, both guys and girls, who would discuss all things sex, love, and relationships. Natasha had a show on the same station entitled "The Build Up Radio." The Build Up was a fun business talk show that interviewed young entrepreneurs about how they managed to build and create brands. Both shows went well into 2011, and it was such a fun experience.

12. Sherrell, April 2010

God,

I cannot believe I even have the guts to do this again after I promised you that I would never do this again. God, its 6 a.m., and I am awake and cannot stop throwing up. I am extremely sick and this is the day that we agreed we would get this abortion done. God, I think I have had enough. I have promised you over and over again that I wouldn't do this again, and here I am back for more torture. For some reason God, I just don't feel as up to doing this as I was in the past. Show me a sign, God. Show me why I shouldn't do this. I know I shouldn't, I know I shouldn't. This one feels different, God. Even though I lock myself in the room, and cannot barely breathe, I want this baby. I know he is going to feel like his life is ending if I have it, but God if this is your will, I have to keep this baby. This baby in my womb is making me uncomfortable and sick, but it also makes me want to know it. The things it's putting me through makes me want to not have this abortion. For some reason, I have already built a bond with this one. God, I have to ask you this: if I have this baby, will it TOTALLY change my life? I mean I hear people say all the time that a baby will turn your life upside down. Well is that what I need? I have lived on the edge and all over the place just because I crave control and the thrill of being on my own terms at all times. But ever since I left my parent's house, something or someone controlled me no matter how I look at it. Is today the day that I make the decision to listen to you wholeheartedly and keep this gift I have been creating for the past few weeks? God, I have killed two babies already. I told you last time that I AM DONE! ......

...

...

...

...

...

...

...

...

"...I'm not going to have the abortion." –ME

"WHAT? Why not? My life is about to be over?" –CK

God, can you believe him? I figured he would feel this way, but I have decided to keep this baby and honor you. I know that this baby is your gift to me and another chance to get my life in order, no matter how much of a mess I am right now. This will also be his wake up call. He is one of the most intelligent men I know. Why doesn't he see that? God, I ask that you protect him and show him that this decision is better for all of us; for him, for me, and for this little baby! Thank you God, for loving and keeping me. I promise to take care of this little baby and love him/her like I have never loved before. God, please cover me during this time of creating and help me to stay close to you. God, please keep Honeycomb Set up and running. God, I know G is going to lose it, but keep us close and connected no matter how fat this little baby makes me. G is spoiled by me. She probably won't be able to handle someone else having all my attention besides her. Protect her too God, and help her to see who she is and what she is MOST capable of. Anyway God, I love this company and the people that are involved. God, you know I am so sick, and I am trying my hardest to do work every day. If it is your will to help my business grow during this time of me creating, then I will follow. This is a life changing moment, and ALL I need is you!

Amen.

For by grace you have been saved through faith. And this is not your own doing; it is the gift of God.
Ephesians 2:8

13. Natasha, 2010

Okay, God. I stepped out on faith and finally quit my full-time job in PA and decided to operate my "cute" little business, (as Ant refers to it) full time. It's funny because I ended up getting two big contracts in one weekend. The first was with a cancer foundation and the second was with a football player's wife. Those two blessings on top of the fact that my annoying coworker printed my Twitter timeline as "proof" that I was tweeting while in our staff meeting sent me over the edge. I quit ASAP. So how nice of my amazing, BOSS boyfriend to invite me to come and stay with him until I found a place. I did. And then, I became really clingy. It wasn't without reason though. Ever since the feds bashed in the door, I had been super paranoid. I'm not sure why *I think* I can protect him, but I would like to.

One day in March, I was getting something out of his trunk, and I saw a little gift bag with a bottle of perfume. I thought it may have been a surprise for me at first, but when he never gave it to me, I knew something wasn't right. Then, he started leaving out of the room to answer calls, or he'd make excuses to go out to "watch the game with the boys," on a Sunday afternoon. One day while he was sleep, I went in the garage and inspected his car, and I found a parking pass to some random apartment complex, a number folded on a white piece of paper, and a card that someone had addressed to him, with a kiss on it. I then broke the one rule he had AGAIN, which was to never go through his phone, and that's when I realized that he wasn't who I thought he was. I was sick, and yet even though I knew I was being disrespected I wasn't ready to give it up yet. I had just left my job to

45

operate my business full time and that relationship was the only sense of security that I had, or so I thought. So I decided to stick it out.

A few months later, we went on a vacation to the ocean, and after that it all fell apart. On July 4th, he decided to take his other girlfriend to Miami or some other exotic city—I assumed it was Miami at the time (maybe because I've made him out to be Rick Ross in my head). But I did investigate his cell records. He always gave me money to pay both of our cell phones from my accounts (because he didn't like anything electronic) so I just called the phone company and requested his records. Then, I called him. The phone picked up. I could tell he was on a boat, because water was splashing in the background—wind muffled the laughter. I thought he was joking when the phone hung up after I heard the female voices. I called back over and over, but there was no answer. Then, at some point, I called and a girl answered. I was stuck.

I started to think about the past few months, the perfume, the phone calls, the whispers, and the text messages that I had seen. That's when it hit me. He was rejecting me, without saying it with words. I'm not one who could deal with rejection well—ever. It pushed me over the edge. I became what most guys in my generation would refer to as "crazy"—excessive calls, pop-up visits in the middle of the night, begging, and pleading for him to take me back and stop breaking my heart. When things had died down, and I knew he was back in town, I drove 45 minutes to his house late at night. *I had to. I just couldn't take the pain anymore.* By this time, I no longer had the code to his gated community, so I parked my car outside of it, then, hopped the fence. I ran all the way through his neighborhood until I was standing outside of his garage.

It was open. *God, why didn't I stop there?*

I went in.

I stood in the garage staring at the door that led to the house.

I turned the knob.

It was unlocked.

I opened it.

The kitchen light was on.

I stepped inside to see if I could hear anything. I didn't.

I silently closed the door behind me, and then, I creeped up the stairs.

I got to the top of the stairs and peeked in the kitchen. I heard snoring.

His son was asleep on the couch, and the NFL network was playing loud through the television.

His son was knocked out. The light was on in Ant's bedroom. I stretched my neck and I saw feet under the covers.

I had a plan. I was going to go in his room, and lie down next to him, and I'd be there when he woke up. He'd be happy to see me, right?

I should have turned around and ran, but I didn't.

I tip-toed through the kitchen, and I stared at his son, making sure that he wasn't watching me.

He was still sound asleep. I kept walking, inching toward the open bedroom door.

When I got to the doorway, I couldn't believe what I was watching. It was like I was in a movie.

I was totally in shock.

There was a knife on his dresser. He collected knives.

I picked it up and opened it.

I stared at him and her lying sound asleep in his bed.

She laid there on MY side of the bed.

She even resembled me, with a black bonnet on her head, sleeping silently and peacefully, like she was *so happy, living my life.*
I looked down at the knife in my hand, and I imagined me stabbing him and then her over and over.

I actually visualized it. I saw their blood all over my hands. The only thing that snapped me out of that moment was a cough. His son coughed.

I put the knife down and hurried out of his room.

I stopped and thought to write a note in red lipstick on the mirror as I had done once before. But then, he'd know I was crazy.

No.

I figured, I'd better just leave.

I hurried out of the living room, through the kitchen, down the stairs, out of the garage, and ran through the neighborhood, hopped the fence and got in my car.

I started crying. Then, I stopped. No more tears could flow.

I decided that I'd call a therapist in the morning.

I am losing it.

The Art of a Woman

Around this time, the two of us were working hard preparing for The Art of a Woman in addition to our other respective client projects. This was to be a major women's empowerment event that would showcase Sherrell's models, including Honeycomb Set's signature model (who later went on to star in *The Bad Girl's Club),* as well as Natasha's visual arts clients. We also had a goal to pull in many of the major female movers and shakers - makeup artists, authors, business women, fashion trailblazers, and more. Natasha was extremely adamant about having one of the top video models in the city host this event. While it wasn't our first time collaborating on our own project, it was definitely the most creative event we produced together. We transformed The District Nightclub in Adams Morgan into an art gallery filled with beautiful women. Everyone loved it!

14. $\mathcal{N}$atasha, Winter, 2011

Ant blocked my phone numbers and cut off the phone he had brought me. I stalked him for a while. He pulled further away. I was heartbroken. I let my finances slip. I let my mortgage and car payments lapse. I slept on my mom's couch for a month, and didn't move—except to use the bathroom. It was over. He no longer cared. My stability was snatched out from under me, and the false sense of self-worth that this relationship gave me was also gone. You know there are five stages of grief—I was bargaining with you, God (later I realized it was not you who controlled me at that moment, but it was Satan. I was actually being controlled by the devil). I thought that if Ant took me back, I'd never be crazy again. I'd be a better girlfriend and I wouldn't go through his phone. It was so pitiful. At first I wondered if I was the only person to suffer so badly from rejection. But I know I'm not alone. I learned rejection is a spirit, you know, and I think this spirit attached itself to me when I was a kid, a stepchild. I have a problem with someone ending something that I'm not ready or hadn't prepared to be over. I have a problem with facing the truth—that some things don't last forever. I know rejection on so many levels, but now I also know why I didn't want to and couldn't accept rejection. So anyway, my depressive, suicidal state lasted for most of last summer. And finally, at the end of August, I was getting back to normal. By September, I was back to myself after several big wins in business. You know Ant even came to my company's anniversary party this year? And guess where it was? The Park of all places! This past year, I've been determined to truly "Boss Up," as my ex-boyfriend tried to teach me.

A year after this whole ordeal, and after a few productive therapy sessions, I was doing PR for an NBA player. This weekend was HUGE! I felt like it was my comeback. I had back-to-back media interviews for my client and my girl Jeannie "Kitty of the City" Jones of 93.9 WKYS shouted me out on the airwaves. She called me Natasha Brown, "Washington's Publicist!" WOW. I so siced. We were celebrating a successful weekend with a charitable benefit at one of the clubs in city. Everyone was there. I felt out of my element, and my social anxiety kicked in. I retreated to the bar, although I had this "No drinking while working" rule. I was standing there, holding up the line of lushes who knew exactly what they wanted to drink. As I contemplated whether or not I'd break my rule to get through the night, I heard his voice say my name. "Natasha."

I smiled, but he couldn't see me. I turned around and it was him. My grin grew and he gave me a hug. He told me great job on the event, and I thanked him. He was back. In an instant, I started to believe in us again. I started to imagine him back in my life. I decided I'd forgive him for treating me so horribly. I wondered where our next "make up" vacation would be, and I envisioned myself back in his place, sitting on his comfy bed, running my business from my laptop while he ran his businesses from his flip phone. Then... he held up his left hand. I froze. I was actually in shock—choking on an imaginary margarita. *Oh how I wish I had ordered that margarita! God, did you send me to that bar to get a drink so that I could brace myself? Why hadn't I just ordered the margarita?* Then his lips started moving. I read them, and knew exactly what he was saying, although all sound around me had stopped.

"I'm married," he said.

I knew that's what he said, because I am good at reading lips. But... I didn't hear him. I felt my face crumble, and my jaws started trembling. I felt the waterworks coming and before anyone else saw what was about to happen, I pushed myself past him, through the packed club straight to the door, and started running as fast as I could, in my heels—up one block, around the corner, and down another block, until I hit the car alarm and swung my door open. Then I screamed out in agony and the tears flooded my steering wheel. Why, how, could he do this to me—after just a year... HE'S MARRIED!?

The temptations in your life are no different from what others experience. And God is faithful. He will not allow the temptation to be more than you can stand. When you are tempted, he will show you a way out so that you can endure.
1 Corinthians 10:13

15. Sherrell, March 2012

Father God in the name of Jesus,

I am so weak right now. My sisters keeping telling me to stop saying it. I love them so much. They keep me so close to you. It amazes me how much my little sisters know so much about your word. I guess because we can sit around and get zooted. Lmsao. Those are some of the best times to talk about you. So we do, and I explain to them that THIS time my thoughts I choose to share with them are not of the usual thoughts I've had in the past. God, I am sharing with them that sometimes I don't feel like I want to be here. I've thought so many times that I just can't do it anymore. God when did this become who I am? However, this is how I feel, so I just thank you for giving me strength to just thank you! My flesh is so weak. Day after day, I find myself giving into temptations. God, I am drinking miniatures on my way to work. I am rushing home to make a drink. I just want to be numb to it all. I don't even want to drink so that I get drunk. Drinking makes me so unaware of all the self-destruction. It's easier to feel another way and mask my pain and my hurt. I'd rather just talk to you about it. People are so quick to judge and I just don't feel like being judged by anyone. I mean I can barely look at myself in the mirror. How can I possibly want to sit and have a conversation with someone about how I am feeling? So I want to just thank you in advance for helping me to stop all the self-destruction. I need to stop drinking, but it's so hard. Fill me up and make me whole again. My actions are speaking a lot louder than my words lately.

51

Meaning, I am late for work almost every day from being so hungover. Not to mention, I am getting so big. The clothes I once could fit laugh at my body for even thinking I could even wear them now. I don't want to "talk" about it to anybody but YOU. I want to just drink the issue away. I feel good when I drown in my own drunkenness. I thank you for delivering me with this. No matter how good it feels, I thank you for casting the enemy and all his tricks away. I thank you for loving me so much to continue listening to me even if I don't hear a response. I will work harder at not drinking my life away. I love you so much God, and I thank you for doing just what you said you would do. God continue to pour into me so that I can be just who my future husband needs. My desire to be AMAZING to him is because those are the desires you poured unto me. I will work that much harder at being obedient. I love you God. In your mighty name I pray, Amen.

July 2012

Father God in the name of Jesus,

Lord, you know I do not want to go to another function. I just want to stay home and drink all day. God, I don't know why I am even apart of such a glamorous group of women when I feel so unattractive. This is the absolute worst time to be a part of this. Are you trying to tell me if I stop drinking I too can be one of these women? I can have a big house and wear expensive shoes and drive really nice cars? I really don't desire all of those things. But the thought crossed my mind. I don't know my lessons from this. It seems more like torture, and it forces me to drink more every day. I am doing business with these women and going out to clubs looking a mess while they are draped in nice clothes and beautiful makeup. God, this addiction to drinking is causing so much turmoil. How am I the one for this job with these women? My story is so different from theirs. Why do you have me here? The more I drink, the more numb I feel. I'd rather be emotionless around them than alert enough to question my material worth to these women. God, I am taking pics with Marsha Ambrosius looking and feeling fat, reeking of alcohol and just so uninterested in being a part of this night. God, I pray that the next time I encounter this woman that I am in a better place. God, please save me and not let her judge me on my current mess. Is this karma for all the times I posted on social media about girls wearing dresses with big stomachs? This feels like I am watching me play a part in a movie as someone else. The only thing is I am not dreaming and this isn't a TV show. This is my reality, and it came at me fast. I am displaying everything I wrote or thought about, and it's taking something like a shift in my appearance to show me that LIFE IS ALWAYS HAPPENING for someone somewhere. I get it now. So please save me from myself and this mess I'm creating. This bottle of alcohol is taking over me and I am allowing it. I need to be released from this prison I have put myself in. I drink to smile. I drink to feed my baby. I drink to laugh. I drink to feel alive at this point, but I always end up feeling numb. How is this living, God? Help me to serve you and only you. I was waiting on you to hear me and give me the sign that your power is much greater than the bottle. HELP ME! Amen.

16. Sherrell, 2012

God, I am so miserable living like this. How did I let someone who was my very best friend turn into someone I cannot stand to see sometimes? The worst part is that I have to live with him forever. God, my mom asked what did I think about marriage with him? I have mixed feelings. I don't think I am in love with him, but I love him. He started as my really good friend. We used to talk about everything and laugh endlessly all night. Now we are both wondering how the other feels. Sometimes being around each other is so uncomfortable. If it wasn't for our baby, we probably would not still be together. I want him to get some help. I need help. I don't think he prays as much as I do. So I want to put in a request to cover my child's father. Show him that he is able.

I can say that things are a little better now. We are now in our "own" place for a second time. God, thank you for removing us from that basement situation. Though it was a blessing to have somewhere to be so that we all were together, that place was the pits. God, you knew that wasn't the place for us to raise our beautiful daughter. It was a bachelor's pad from the first night I was there. I cleaned that room from top to bottom, but overall, it was still a place for a man to cave, not for a family with a newborn. However, we stayed because it was convenient and we had no responsibility to stay there. I mean we had to pay a cable bill here and there, but no real obligations. There was nothing to push us out. Until the basement began to flood and mold and mildew started to form. I immediately began searching for single family home basements, because the owners were more likely to let us rent, without an extensive credit check. I have always ran from that, and God you know that there was no way I was about to start facing my credit issues. I just couldn't. He was working a temp job while I was in Baltimore working. I hate this job, God. It is the worst. I am too creative for a nine to five, especially this one. Please remove me from this place.

The bills here are becoming overwhelming, and CK isn't working anymore, God. I don't know if we can stay here any longer. God, please? Where will we go? Is this our time to go our separate ways? I know he doesn't want that, but I feel like we should. God, what do we do?

Okay, we are at his mom's house and we told her we just need two weeks, and we would have another place. I KNEW that timing was not realistic. We had no money saved up and my credit was a mess. God, please what should I do? It's no way I can stay here. I got it. I am going to call Joe to see if we can come stay with him. I know he wouldn't mind. Plus this will probably help him. He is not in the best state right now since he can't see JJ. He hasn't been himself since all this stuff transpired with his baby mother keeping her from him.

Thank you, God! Gabby and I are going to stay with Joe, and CK will stay here with his mom. CK does NOT like this idea, but this is what it is. We agreed to co-parent. He gets Gabby every other week and so do I. This way she sees us both all the time. I hate to do this to her, but this has to happen! Thanks God for always looking out for me and answering my prayers.

Amen.

Okay Ladies,

This is 2016 Natasha.

Time and again, I found myself mending the pieces of my broken heart back together, because I gave myself away too easily. This sad story of mine repeated itself over and over during my twenties. I gave myself away over and over, looking for someone who'd love me for me and accept me as broken and confused as I was. The truth is, nobody could deal with that. I was a mess, and even my "hero" Ant, (or so I thought, who tried his hardest to save me) couldn't deal with it. Once he found someone who was actually mature and who acted her age, he kicked me to the curb. But because I really was a diamond (who didn't realize it yet), and I was smart with business savvy, he nor any other man wanted to just be upfront with me. They all wanted to keep me around because I was good for their businesses. They also figured I was too preoccupied with my business and my clients to dedicate time to being a private detective who would stop at nothing to know the truth. *Lord knows I should have been too busy for their bull.* But I wasn't. Soon, I made a habit of using my intelligence, power, and connections for bad, instead of the millions of other productive ways I could've been building an empire for myself, and becoming a true boss. My disdain for rejection, breakups, and heartbreak led me down a toxic, terrible, and near deadly path that almost landed me in jail on many occasions—

In part 2, you'll learn more about what finally set me straight. But let me just say that after I published my book, *10 Blessings of Betrayal,* in 2015 and began working with trauma survivors, I realized why I had so many issues with relationships. During this time, I learned that trauma victims often stop developing emotionally at the age when they suffer from the trauma. Unless they (or better yet we) deal with what happened to us in the past, we simply stay STUCK. This bit of knowledge began to open up so many areas of understanding for me. Were both Sherrell and I "trauma" survivors? Did we stop developing mentally, in our personal emotional lives? Why was I, personally, so immature? I'd started having sex early. I had been raped at 15. I was forced to have an abortion at 17. And as I began to look at my life through this lens, I realized that I had traumatized myself and had been damaged by others over and over and over up until my early thirties. I'd let other people define my worth—men, clients, family, flings, friends. Up until that point, I hadn't viewed myself from the lens that God viewed me. I was a SLAVE and victim to the world and my business, but not to God. I had never gotten help or talked to anyone about the real issues that had been hurting me. This vicious cycle started in my teens, and I'd suffered silently through so much pain, and sought love in the wrong places for almost 20 years of my life. I tried to mend my true hurts through academics, accomplishments, and entrepreneurial and career achievements. I overcompensated for my insecurities and the fear I had of rejection by depending instead on the things that I knew would help me gain acceptance. I tried to make my "works" speak for me—work in the community and in my career. I thought that these "works" would make me feel accepted and loved. The problem is, this wasn't a sustainable plan. I didn't know my self-worth. I didn't know God's word, and therefore I didn't have faith that I could do all things through Christ, because He and He alone is my strength.

I didn't know God, and so God made me wait. I meet so many people today in my work who remind me of me. I see it so clear—they're geniuses who lack self-love, and they are unable to accept rejection and unable to reject the BS that is threatening to steal their futures. After we understand these things, we must reject them and accept us. And we must separate from all things toxic. Separation happens on three levels: in our mental, spiritual, and physical beings. When we fail to learn the lesson the first time, we keep suffering through the same tests over and over again. And we keep turning back and going in circles, until we finally crash and burn.

This is 2016 Sherrell.

God said not to dwell, but to be still in His will. I have learned to understand that God may not always respond like the flesh when you need Him, but He is always listening. God never left me during the times mentioned in part one of this book. He gave me exactly what I needed when I needed it; he covered me and kept me living. I put myself through so much turmoil and blamed any and every one for me not being successful in relationships, in business, and everything else. However, I recognized that I was not living right. I saw that my actions led me into situations that were not of God. God kept me EVERY day. You just read my thought process during those times. I ONLY consulted with God with the fear of being judged by my unsettling decisions. I always went to God with a genuine heart, an obedient spirit, it was flesh that was my issue. I didn't allow God to renew my mind fully, so that he could give me a new perspective on how my heart should feel and what it should desire. I was broken and a mess. I forced myself to be someone I really wasn't. I created an illusion, and because I introduced this illusion to the world I had to keep it going no matter how much self-destruction I was causing. That was so INSANE of me. I know a lot of you reading this can identify with people-pleasing and looking for validation from people that cannot help you get to your final destination. I had to confront the demons that were behind closed doors and in my face causing so much ruckus while God was showing me to be still and wait on Him, to let Him handle it. The INSANE part was I knew that God wasn't pleased with my actions. I talked about it to Him all the time. But until you make up your own mind to stop the self-torture and destruction, you'll never be ready to receive the many blessings that God has.

I knew God was a miracle worker, but the world had a tight grip on my flesh and it was so hard to let go of what made my flesh feel good. My soul and spirit cried out for help daily and often every hour. Sometimes life takes you through a tragic situation to show you how valuable your life is, but even more so how important it is to have God in your life and to honor him.

GOD MADE ME WAIT!

In Part 2, I will show you how my life took a turn for the worst after having my beautiful baby girl, Gabriella. I will show you how I made a decision to slow down and give myself to God piece by piece. It shows you how awesome God is and how He NEVER leaves you even in your mess. It shows that He has written our story beautifully and perfectly for us, even in our mess. God has blessed me time and time again, and has proven His power in my life's trials, tribulations, and WINS. I pray that what you take away from this book is not to glorify your sin, but to own it and pray for forgiveness and healing so that God can bless you abundantly and you can live life like a true champion!!!

Part 2

PLAN.

Give it ALL to God.

"And as they brought them out, one said, "Escape for your life. Do not look back or stop anywhere in the valley. Escape to the hills, lest you be swept away."
Genesis 19:17

Lot was the nephew of Abraham, whose story is shared in Genesis 19. The Lord warned Lot and his wife to leave the destructive city of Sodom and Gomorrah, and in the above verse, they were warned NOT TO LOOK BACK OR STOP. After they left, Lot thought everything was cool. Why wouldn't it be? God delivered his family from doom and planned to give him a new start in new territory. It would have been an amazing escape, except Lot's wife could not resist the urge to see what was happening in their former home. She looked back and turned into a pillar of salt (verse 26). Lot then witnessed "the smoke of the land which went up like the smoke of a furnace." God destroyed the cities, but he remembered Abraham, and because of the favor on Abraham's life, he sent Lot out of the midst of the destruction. There are quite a few lessons packed within this story, but the one we'll focus on here is the danger of looking back or returning to the places we've been delivered from. There is a reason that God delivers us, protects us, sends us dreams-visions-warning signals that tell us to stop or turn around, don't look back, and to simply move forward! Unfortunately, many of us women don't take those signals. We instead depend on our own knowledge and give in to the temptation to return to the familiar, just as Lot's wife did.

For the people who say God does not save or know sinners, you don't know God like we know God. No one can take what God has done for us (or you for that matter), or what he has in store. This book is a release. We are finally releasing the past, and we are ready for the future. But before we wrote this, we had to pray and ask, "God, is this the message that you want us to relay? Do you really want us to dig deep into our past and show how much we sinned or how much we ran?" God has been using us for years separately and collectively. Why wouldn't we share how devastating it was to lean on our own understanding while still praying to God? Leaving the ways of the world and our temptation to return to that familiar thing is hard to do. You face being judged, disowned, ridiculed, and bashed by the people you once ran the streets with. More often than not, once you turn from your past transgressions you will be condemned by the good, ol' holier than thou church folks who have "never" sinned a day in their lives. But you may also be judged by the people from your past life. Since we cannot please everyone, we might as well live for God, right?

We learned early on that the ones in the church who judge you or condemn you about owning your past are the ones running from theirs. So we couldn't dare let the fact that they may try and doom us to hell stop us from showing the realness of God's power and loyalty to His people. We are now unafraid to show you the way the enemy works diligently in our lives to destroy us and make us the laughing stock in hell. We are no longer slaves to the enemy. Now don't confuse this, we still sin. We are not holier than thou. However, we know the value in honoring God and not worshipping and glorifying our sins. We work on rectifying situations that may cause us to become employees of Satan, and we pray our way into the work of God. By this we use our past to fuel our fire for God. The fire that makes us powerful worshippers through singing, ministry, and spreading His word through our most transparent moments. Watch how God uses us. Once God delivers you, it's so important not to look back unless you are doing so to heal or lift others up.

And they overcame him by the blood of the Lamb, and by the word of their testimony; and they loved not their lives unto the death.
Revelation 12:11

17. Sherrell, January 2013

Omgoodness, God what am I doing here? How did I end up here? Why would I wait to have my beautiful baby to end up on my near death bed? Who brought me here? Why am I hooked up to so many cords? What happened? No one is here to explain to me what happened? God, CAN YOU HEAR ME? WHAT IS HAPPENING?

"Hello, Ms. Woodward. How are you feeling?" It was a nurse, in what looked like scrubs to perform surgery.

"Wait, I'm in the hospital for what? Why am I here? Did I pass out? Where is my daughter? Does anyone know that I'm here? Can you answer me, lady?" I didn't give this woman one chance to answer me. What could have possibly happened? God, whatever it was, did you decide to save me AGAIN?

Okay, I get it. I have to stop drinking. God, the doctor came in here to tell me that I passed out and had to be given seven bags of IV fluid in order to get my body to a normal hydration level. My blood pressure had skyrocketed, and I was so dehydrated that my left pupil was closed solid. God, have I really caused this much damage to myself? I am now living with my brother in his one bedroom, with a den, and I can no longer attribute *my* drinking to Gabby's dad. It is ALL me. I am doing this to myself. I have to let it go. I know you sent me to live with my brother for a reason, and in order for me to take this assignment, I have to stop drinking and get my life in order. God, I have gained over 100 pounds just from all the horrible things I have put in my body. I am scared for Gabby, God. I know she is our pre-

62

cious gift and our reason to be better people. I want to give her the world. As soon as I leave this hospital I am going to call my brother Sam and ask him to help me to lose this weight. I'm sure he would be more than happy to do it.

Today is the day God. Thank you so much for giving me the strength to transform into a healthier me. I spoke with Sam, and God he is so pumped, and I am not ready to deal with his shenanigans lmsao. But to be honest, I am so glad that I am doing this with Sam. He has looked out for me since I was 10 years old, running around Riverdale asking all the hustlers for money. Sam would always see me and tell me to "stop asking niggas for money." He always made sure I had enough cash to last me, so I wouldn't have to ask anybody for anything. He has been looking out for me for years, and I trust him with my life. He has made that previous statement come to light on multiple occasions, but I won't get into that.

Okay Lord, I am here at the gym and I am ready. I walked into the gym and told Sam I am going to take a picture of myself and post it on Instagram. Sam didn't want me to do it, because he was afraid of the back-lash I would get since I had gotten so big. God, I can't believe that Sam is displaying any inkling of fear. This is why I know I have to post this picture. He kept going on and on about the bruises on my arm from them sticking me in the hospital and that I don't want the world to see me like this, but I didn't care. I am ready to break free from the self-destruction. God, if this is your will, put it in my heart to post freely through my entire journey. I thank you for using me to possibly help millions of other women who are in my situation. I thank you for using me in advance. I thank you for giving me the slogan #TheGoodThick to help hold myself accountable. I will not let you down. CONTINUE TO STAY WITH ME!

God, I make a vow to you that, from this day forward, I will not drink myself into a coma and I will value your power and unconditional love. I thank you for using Sam to help me to evolve into this new woman you have created me to be. Here we go!

I find rest in God;
only he gives me hope.
He is my rock and my salvation.
He is my defender;
I will not be defeated.
My honor and salvation come from God.
He is my mighty rock and my protection.
People, trust God all the time.
Tell him all your problems,
because God is our protection.
Psalm 62:5-8

18. Natasha, February 2013

God, I thank you for bringing me/us through that summer of terror, but we've entered the coldest winter ever, and I don't know what to do. I started something new. I'm determined to read the Bible app every morning, and maybe I can finish this One Year Bible plan too. Even though we're crammed in this basement room together, both extremely miserable, with no car and no real money, I am happy to be learning so much about you through your word. I go outside in the backyard, with my coffee every morning, sit on the steps, and read. It's the only thing I have right now. My relationship is miserable. Business, on the outside looks great. I've won a couple of awards for PR, despite this very dark season. I thank you for continuing to boss me up on the outside, even if I'm crumbling on the inside. One day, I pray that my entire life can be on display for you to show the world what you've done.

So at first, I thought you brought JD and I back together last year because "we were meant to be." He understood me and accepted my past. I could actually be real with him, about *everything* I've done, and he promised not to hold it against me. It also seemed like he and I both truly changed over the three years that passed. There were still so many feelings we had from 2009 too. But then I learned that we were both broken.

On July Fourth of last year, however, everything changed. He was helping me fix so much drama that my client, a reality show star from *Real Hip-Hop*, was causing surrounding the logistics of her "celebrity" weekend in DC. She seemed to be fond of the way JD spoke to her (he has this amazing charm), so I let him calm her down. We were at my brother's beach house working, getting drunk, eating, and having a party with dozens of the closest people to me. I fell asleep, and woke up to him yelling at me about not saving enough food for him. I was so confused, and I tried to calm him down. I'd never seen him behave like this. We'd been having an amazing few months since we got back together. He was getting louder and my family was right downstairs, so I suggested that we go outside. As I was walking down the stairs in the front of the house, he pushed me. I tumbled down several stairs and fell to the concrete. When my brothers came out, and said they knew he pushed me, I denied it. That turned out to be a very bad decision. *Lord, what would have happened if I had just told the truth? Maybe there would have been a fight or worse - one of the men I love could have gotten hurt. I didn't want that to happen, so I lied. I sacrificed myself.*

In the following days, we went to Stadium, for the reality TV client's event, and afterwards, we got in this huge fight in the car, and he banged my head against the window. He almost crashed. God, thanks for saving me. It was such a close call.

For my birthday in August, we planned this huge, all-white pool party at my mom's house. The party was crazy! My client was DJing and JD was performing a new song. That was the last semi-happy moment that I can remember. I think the pressure from losing so much money really pushed him over the edge. We took $15,000 out of my bank account, and we were going to flip it. But we kept spending and spending and making poor choices with money.

The summer of terror continued. The next week, he ran over my dog Honey, which we've had for nearly twenty years, and killed her. He said it was an accident. Then, the following weekend, he went ballistic. Ant's man, C (who owns the computer shop and who has been like a big brother to me since I was seeing Ant) was fixing the laptop that JD broke during one of his rants. I guess JD got tired of me complaining, so he made me get in the car, and he drove to C's shop and tried to kick in the door and threatened to kill him unless he hurried up and fixed my computer. Someone must've seen this and called the police. The next thing I know, the Capitol Police were chasing us. They pulled us over, and JD got locked up. We waited a few hours downtown, and they let him go. That night, we went back to his mom's house where we were staying, and he completely *flipped!*

Okay, I know that there must be something special that you plan to do with my life, because you have saved me too many times. I can't believe that he threatened me with a knife, made me get in a suitcase, zipped it up, and threatened to throw the suitcase in the Anacostia River. What in the hell? His sister and mother were home, and I overheard him arguing with them. Next thing I know, he was screaming to the top of his lungs. I can't remember how I got out of that suitcase, but when I did, he was running, crying and hollering. His face was turning red like fire, and it was the first time that he looked like a demon to me. His sister Maced him to calm him down! I felt so sorry for him, and I wanted to take his pain away. He was literally crumbling in front of my eyes. He made me grab my things and get in the car. I fidgeted around the house, trying to take as much of my things as I could. Something told me I wouldn't be allowed back there. The entire time, he was burning up from the fumes, crying, screaming, threatening me, telling me that I didn't love him, while begging me to never leave him. With all of that happening, he was also directing me where to drive. He had me go up-town to his old neighborhood and then to Southeast to a house where his dad (who has been dead for years) lived. He wanted to go past the cemetery where he was buried, and we also drove past Anacostia Park. I kept praying that the idea of throwing me in the river wouldn't return to his mind.

Lord, what have I gotten myself into? When we got back to his mom's house, the place was empty. The next day, when we woke up, all I could think to do was to get him to North Carolina, because his daughter's first day of school was the next day. He had never missed her first day, so I figured that her presence could calm him down. God, I honestly feel so bad for him. I did not experience what he did as a child, and I truly just want him to get help. I really do think we could have a positive future if he does.

August 2012

This is the realist thing I've ever heard.

When he tells you, "'Baby fuck it, let's die together,'" you just remember that you were born alone and you will die alone."
I just started praying silently and asked You to save our lives. And that moment is exactly when he took my wheel, as we were driving south on 95 and tried to run the car directly into a tractor trailer. *"Oh my God, oh my*

God, please save me!"

Not sure if this was the best idea or not, but I LOST it. Gave him a piece of his own medicine. I looked over at him and his eyes were bulging out of his head. He was burning and shaking from the fire he had felt from being Maced by his foster sister. When I saw him, and that determination of death in his eyes, I flipped.

"AHHHHHH," I Screamed! TO THE TOP OF MY LUNGS, I JUST STARTED SCREAMING! Then I jerked the wheel really hard, so he let it go, and I nearly ran us into the little, red compact car that was approaching on the passenger side - his side of the car.

"YOU WANT TO DIE? FINE! LET'S FUCKING DIE — TO-GETHER! YOU GO FIRST!" I shouted and tried to hit the car with everything I had.

"Oh, you think you're fucking crazy, now, huh?" he said. "Are you trying to kill me? Huh? You want me dead too?"

"YOU SAID YOU WANT TO DIE? SO FUCK IT! LET'S DIE. RIGHT HERE, THREE HOURS BEFORE GOING TO SEE YOUR DAUGHTER FOR THE LAST TIME. LET'S FUCKING DIE!!!!! I'M TIRED OF THIS BULLSHIT. WHAT DID I DO TO YOU? WHY ARE YOU DOING THIS??? I CAN'T TAKE IT ANYMORE. I'D RATHER US DIE THAN PUT UP WITH ANOTHER MINUTE OF YOUR PSYCHOTIC BULLSHIT!" Of course I wanted to live. But I've learned that sometimes, you have to deal with psychopaths with the same thing they use on you - reverse psychology.

"YOU want to know why I'm doing this? Because I don't give a fuck anymore. I've fucking lost it. We're going to die today," he assured me.

At that moment, in the middle of interstate traffic, my car began to stall. Then it slowed down. We were in the fast lane, all the way to the left. The car slowed down, slowed down, slowed down...

"WHAT'S HAPPENING?! BABE WHAT'S GOING ON, WHY ARE YOU SLOWING DOWN?"

"I'M NOT!! IT'S THE CAR. IT'S FEELS LIKE IT'S STOPPING. IT WON'T ACCELERATE." I had no idea what was happening.

At this point, I think we were both thinking a bit more logically.

God, the only thing I do in this basement is replay these moments from the summer of terror. These memories keep haunting me.

He must increase, but I must decrease.
John 3:30

19. Sherrell, May 2013

Yesssssss God! I am down 40 pounds since January. I can feel you working on me EVERY day. I am loving the new me. God, I thank you so much for giving me the strength to stop drinking. Lord, you know that was one of the worst habits I carried over the last year and a half. However, I do thank you for STILL covering my flesh. Since I haven't been with CK it's been a whirlwind with my sexual life. I am finding myself dealing with a few of the guys that I was with in the past. God, why do I feel I need to go back to them? I hate being single. It always shows how weak my flesh is. It shows how weak I am and how disobedient I am to your word. Then I think you'll forgive me, once I repent. God, there can't be any real growth in that. *deep sigh* God, I just thank you for continuing to renew my mind. Now that the drinking has stopped, I can hear and even feel your presence more. I am definitely nothing like I used to be. However, since I am not in a stable relationship, I get a little promiscuous. I don't know why I feel like sex is always the answer.

I think it all started in Summer '97 when I lost my virginity. God I was only thirteen years old. Why was I so sexually attracted to this seventeen year old? I use to stand on the front porch of our apartment complex either awaiting his return or his departure, just so I can see or smell him. God, when I think about it, it scares me to know that at thirteen years YOUNG I was and THIS involved with my sexuality. What has happened to make me even tap into these feelings? God, I just thank you in advance for covering Gabriella and shielding her from a promiscuous lifestyle. God, I beg of you to stop the enemy's plan to destroy my daughter's life. She doesn't deserve this curse. Let her deal with her own issues not the bad choices I made. She shouldn't have to suffer from my burdens. She is so special, protect her.

Anyway God, I know I am not going to change overnight, but I am really hard on myself especially now since I am more aware of you and how you are working in my life. I just pray that you send me one man who will love me unconditionally, cherish the ground I walk on, love me as you do, and that will always make me feel like I am dreaming. God, this will be my prayer each and every day. I thank you for continuing to work in me and using me to reach your people. I see you working.

GOD!!!! I can't believe I just gave him my number. Is this you? Is this him? Am I moving too fast? God, Black Boo hasn't reached out to me in years. I wonder if he is single. The last time we talked was in 2007, when he drove me home because Eddie couldn't. Back then, Black was in a relationship. Well, I gave him my number. I have always thought our conversations were cool. But how ironic is it that he sends me this message the day after I ask you to send me this man that can love me in all those ways? Okay God, let me chill before I have sex with him and mess it up.

Oh God, he IS in a relationship uuuuugggggghhhhh!!! Why him? Is this a test? We have some really great conversations, and I think I am really starting to like him, but God I know this is wrong, because if I were his girl, I would be pissed to know that he was talking to someone that may possibly like him or be interested. I am going to send him a message telling him that we can no longer talk, because this is not right, and I refuse to be anyone's side chick. Thank you God, but no thank you!
Amen.

June 2013

Yesssss I am so excited, God! My homegirls and I are going on a trip to Puerto Rico. I have never been there before, and I am so pressed to show off all of my hard work on my body. I have changed my eating habits. I haven't had one ounce of alcohol, and I haven't missed one workout. I am now down 55 pounds and ready to have a ball with my girls. God, I thank you for protecting my flesh and blocking any and all things that are not of you before I go on this trip. Maybe you will even introduce me to a man that can value me as a woman. A man that will see my true worth underneath all of my brokenness. A man that values himself and puts you first. I know every time I pray to you lately it's about my Prince Charming. Lmsao GOD, I just am tired of being lonely and for some reason, I cannot stop thinking about Black. I haven't talked to him since that last time I told him that I couldn't talk to him anymore. I have never felt like this about any man. Why can't I get him off my mind? What is it about him that intrigues me? Well I do pray that he is okay. I remember last time he was saying he wasn't quite happy. Well, I ask that if he is not happy where he is, to remove or rekindle. I know this is selfish of me, but if he doesn't rekindle that relationship, I thank you in advance for him calling me first lmsao. It's funny because I never see him post about relationships. I wonder... never mind, God. I'll just focus on this trip and let you deal with that whole Black situation.

Oh no! Well, I know NOTHING is going to happen on this trip, being as though I always get my period when I travel. Why does this happen? Okay God, I won't question you this time. I just thank you for protecting me from my own flesh because this dark chocolate man I just met here on the beach is feeling me, and I am feeling him. I don't even know why. He's not attractive at all, but he has this swag about him that is to die for. He reminds me of "The Beast" from my favorite show "Beauty and the Beast." He is turning me completely on with the way he talks, because he's from Jersey and it's just so sexy. I mean he REALLY looks like a BEAST. Why am I even giving him the slightest idea that he can hit, God? Please stop me while I am ahead.

Whew! God, you go so hard. Thank you for stopping that episode in his hotel room. I know my friends are like 'Where is she?' I took a cab over to his hotel to "have some drinks and talk," but it ended up with him trying to penetrate me in my butt SMH. Such a messy situation. God, I am so ashamed. I am so glad I made a run for it by saying I felt sick, and I was going to throw up. Well he was ending his time with me there. He and his friend rode back to our hotel with me because "they liked our beach better" and they wanted to drink and eat with us. This guy wasn't so bad after he found out that sex with me wasn't happening. We took some pictures on the beach, ate, and had a GRAND time. Somehow God, I still cannot get Black off of my mind.

Though I was missing him, I did something to spite him, to see if his cool, calm, collected demeanor would budge. I posted a picture of me and "The Beast" on IG with a caption that read "Have I found my Beast?" Well God, thanks a lot. That plan backfired BAD! CK called me and asked me was I losing my mind posting pictures on IG with other men, and how could I embarrass him. So this was a shock to me, because it was then that I realized that he still had hope for us getting back together. I loved him so much but I couldn't be in another intimate relationship with him. He was dealing with too much hurt and rage, while my spirit was trying to heal from all that has happened to me. I was ready to give myself to you God, and he just wasn't for it or maybe he would have been if I gave him the chance to change with me. God he always said, "I ran." He was right. I just couldn't go back to that place I was in when I was with him. I just didn't like who I had become. So it was more so me needing to heal than not wanting to be with him. The two didn't seem like they would work hand-in-hand. So now, I have to deal with his rage. God, you know when CK gets going, it is no stopping him. We are both very passionate, emotional, aggressive people so that conversation was one for the books. Nevertheless, CK and I finally called it quits. It hurt, but it was needed. I asked him if we could please remain friends for the sake of my heart and for Gabby. That didn't sit well with him, and I could tell, but he went with it just "for the sake of it."

After all of that, Black never mentioned the picture. Dag God, what do I have to do to move this man? He's different huh? My old antics aren't going to work? I have to change and be better to me in order for him to pursue me fully. I am willing to do that for this man. How do I feel so deeply connected to him already? God, what are you up there doing?? Whatever it is, continue to stay with me!

Amen.

> *When you forgive this man, I forgive him, too. And when I forgive*
> *whatever needs to be forgiven, I do so with Christ's authority for your*
> *benefit, so that Satan will not outsmart us. For we are familiar with*
> *his evil schemes.*
> **2 Corinthians 2:10-11**

20. Natasha, 2013

Some of the last words that Ant said to me when we broke up were, "Shorty, don't ever question yourself. You know what you know, and when you feel like something is up, it is. You're smarter than you think. Don't ever let a nigga play you."

God, every time I look at my face in the mirror, I burn with a need to get revenge for what he's done to me. I think that I completely hate JD. I'm being played and it's a different kind of game. How could he be so cold to me? No, we haven't fought in a while, but it's like he does nothing while I grind my ass off to take care of us both. He just sits on the left side of the bed, *all day* playing a stupid Candy Crusher game on his phone. Every hour, he goes outside and paces around the background and smokes a Black & Mild, then sits back down on the bed and plays that stupid game. Granted, I know he's had a rough couple of years, but so have I. I've tried to be compassionate. I was supportive of him the entire time he was locked up, and I held us down and got us a place while he was behind bars. Part of me feels bad because he's so used to hustling and I know he feels like a fish out of water when he can't do that. I think about telling him to leave all the time, but there's no way I can be disloyal. Loyalty is everything. I want to hold him down. So I sit in the bed, working on my laptop all day. I sometimes have to go out for meetings, and so I've been catching the bus or getting rides from friends and clients. I really hate him, and I hate that because of him, my family no longer loves me. No one talks to me except my mom. And I honestly can't stand her either. She made this situation so much worse by posting things about him and his business on Facebook and Twitter, sending out emails and calling him so much. I know she loves me and she was only doing what she could think to do in order to protect me, but did you know that he got locked up because of her? Then she sent me to a psych ward twice. She says she did all these things because she loves me. WHATEVER. I'm not seventeen anymore, and she cannot control what I do with my body anymore either. I can't believe her, and she has the audacity to call me every week like I'll ever forgive her. I can't stand her. I just want her to love me the way I need to be loved. I don't want to be controlled by anyone else. I miss my sister, my brothers, my niece, and my nephew. But I hate them for not understanding and getting mad at me for not leaving him. Okay, I don't hate my niece and nephew. LOL. Let me simmer down. My family just doesn't understand that *I could not leave!* I even miss Mac. I can't believe that JD got in a fistfight with him. Who fights their girlfriend's dad? I just can't believe that I am still with him. Every day, besides reading your word and working on my computer, I replay the summer of terror over and over in my head and I secretly plot on how I am going to break this off with him and make him feel the pain I feel. But then, I feel guilty for having those thoughts. *How will I ever forgive him, God?*

I replay the day when our car broke down on the way to North Carolina. I know that was you working on my behalf. In between all of my cursing and anger I was praying that you would make him stop acting crazy, and you made the car stop. I know that you exist, God. What else could have made the car stop like that? You saved my life that day, I'm sure of it, and I thank you. I just can't wait until I'm out of this situation. I can't wait until we can move from this basement. I think that if we lived someplace else it would be so much better. We have a gay male roommate, who we have to share a bathroom with, and JD hates that with all of his heart. He's so miserable here, and I understand. Our other roommate is an old disabled veteran who lives upstairs, and he chain smokes cigarettes, which I can smell through the vents. I'm so tired of this place but once again, I know this was a blessing from you. I tried to go back home to my mom's once JD got locked up, but she found out I was trying to see him, then she found my safe and tried to break into it, and so I knew I immediately had to get out of there. Thank God for Craigslist and this room I found for $500. Me and JD had been to five of our friends' houses in a month, and we had to leave each one, because of our fights and the police being called. I'm not sure why I felt like we were both on the run. I should have just went to all of my friends' houses by myself, instead of bringing him along with me. I should have known that he wouldn't change. Maybe this is like my wilderness of preparation, similar to how you had to prepare the Jews by taking them through Exile.

$\mathcal{N}$atasha, 2013

Okay, God so first things first! Thanks for making the Get Kids Movin' Tour! pop. Our event at the National Harbor was amazing and so was the event at The Boulevard. I pulled in all my talented folks to help out with it, and NBC caught wind, and we were featured on television… and guess who they interviewed?! You are so dope, God. Thank you for making me so smart and talented, and thank you for sending me amazing and talented clients who I can vibe and be creative with. Thank you for not taking my gifts away, despite my sin. Wow. How could one girl live such a double life? I wish I could live in the amazing highs of my career every second. But when I'm in this basement, all I do is replay the summer of terror back in my head. Maybe your word is showing me a different perspective on things. I am starting to see how you were with me all along, even though I was going through hell. I am also seeing how our pride and brokenness caused our self-destruction.

That night the car broke down, we got back to his mom's house, and we were met by the police and restraining orders, not to enter her home again. So we went to my friend Key's house. The car broke down again on the way there, and she came to get us. The next day, when Key went to work, he started acting crazy again. He was threatening me, and he pushed me. We started arguing in her backyard, and I was so nervous that the neighbors would hear. He was all up in my face yelling at me, and then he just head butted me so hard that my skull split open. Blood started gushing every-where, and I felt the air entering my head and my skin dangling off of my face. I was screaming frantically, and then he started freaking out. He had a knife in his hand that he had been waving in my face and holding up to my neck.

Then God, I think this was you interfering again. God, I know this was you, because at that moment this idiot stabbed himself in the leg with the damn knife. I was screaming from the pain in my head and still trying to find a bandage that would stop the bleeding. He was screaming from stab-bing himself, and then, he demanded that I call the ambulance, because he thought he was dying. He had been shot before in the same leg, so he thought *he was dying*. I have never ever dealt with such a punk ass bitch. As much shit as he's put me through, and he couldn't take a little stab in his leg. He wouldn't show me, so I'm sure it wasn't that serious either. SMH. So I called 911. He kept shouting, "Tell them don't send the police. Send the ambulance and hurry. Bitch, do you hear me? Tell them no fucking police. If the police come, I will kill you, I promise."

Then he asked me what they were saying. The 9-1-1 operator was asking me all sorts of questions by this point.

"Ma'am. What's your name? Ma'am, what is he saying?"

"He said don't send the police, send the ambulance," I repeated over and over again *as if she was dumb, to give her a hint that I needed help, and fast!*

"Ma'am is anyone hurt?"

"PUT THE DAMN PHONE ON SPEAKER, BITCH!" he yelled.

"Ma'am don't put me on speaker. Are you okay? Are there weapons?"

I started giving her yes or no answers, and I kept stalling. This operator would be my witness. Meanwhile, JD was telling me to dump the weed in the toilet.

"Ma'am can you hear me? We are sending you help. Stay on the phone okay?"

"HANG UP THE PHONE! DID THEY SAY THEY ARE SENDING AN AMBULANCE? I'M DYING!"

"Yes, babe." I tried to keep calm and talk slowly as I plotted out my next move.

"HANG UP THE PHONE NOW!"

I kept the phone on, but I put it down so that if he killed me the police would know what happened. All I could do was think about how to save myself. Once JD thought the cops were off the phone and the police were not coming, he proceeded to threaten me.

"Babe, listen to me. You need to go and comb your bang over your forehead, and put a Band-Aid on it right now."

A BAND-AID? MY HEAD WAS GASHED IN TO THE SKULL. Blood had already seeped through several towels, and the kitchen floor was covered in blood.

"Listen, babe. Babe, are you listening? Here's what you need to do. If you don't follow my instructions to a t-we will both go to jail for a very long time, you hear me? You have to put a bandage on your head. When the ambulance gets here, tell them you do not want to go to the hospital. You are okay. I need you to go to the car, and get everything out of the car. You know what I have in there. You need to clean up this mess. Bitch, if you mess this up, I promise I will kill you. Do you hear me?"

God, I'm not sure how I remained so calm. He was bleeding from his leg. I was bleeding from my head profusely. I was getting so weak. I hadn't eaten and had been living off of a coffee and cigarette diet for the past several days. As I was trying to follow all of his frantic instructions, I saw tons of movement in the backyard. After that, the scene got even crazier. About eight cops bombarded us through the backdoor in the kitchen and they were pointing long guns that looked like rifles.

This scene was all too familiar, I thought. They searched the whole house, and didn't find anything illegal. Then they went to my car. I panicked, remembering that I never made it out there. They came back in, and said they were taking my car and computer, and they'd be escorting us both to the hospital. They found drugs in the car. So my car was impounded along with my livelihood, the computer.

They took us both to the hospital in separate ambulances. I got in the hospital room, and was so thankful for this bed. It felt like forever since I'd slept on a comfortable bed. After a while, the voice of a female doctor woke me up. She was there to stitch up my forehead. The tall, beautiful, blonde physician began to tell me that I was being abused, and she'd seen so many women like me who are unfortunately not alive anymore.

"Ma'am, this is your chance to leave. You can talk to the police and tell them what he did to you, and you won't get in trouble. He's still in the other room. We're almost done stitching his wounds. You don't have a lot of time to waste. You have to speak up now or you may die." She told me to consider my options and she left.

After that, a cop came in my room to question me. He told me that they found several pills and illegal narcotics in my car and they could charge me with possession and intent to distribute.
"Listen ma'am. I know that these drugs are not yours. All you have to do is tell us that they aren't yours, and they're his. We know that you are being abused, and we want to help you. We want to help you. I can help you if you just tell me everything you know. How big is your boyfriend's drug operation? Who else is involved?"

Lord have mercy!! I was pissed. Here I am running for my life, and this cop is trying to get me to snitch. I refused to talk to him. He said he'd give me a moment, and he'd be back.

I disregarded him. I was more so thinking about what the doctor said. Her words stung. *"You have to speak up now or you may die."* I believed her. I knew that I would be dead in a week, given everything I'd been through just that weekend. I knew I had to leave. When I opened my eyes, she was back.

"He just got released and he's waiting in the lobby for you. I can still have him arrested. I can have someone come and pick you up and take you to a shelter or we can get you a ride home."

When she said "ride," I remembered that I no longer had a car. I was in another county, and it seemed like I was far away from home. I didn't even know the name of this hospital or how much it would cost to get home from here. My family had disowned me. I had $32 in my pocket. My computer was gone, and with all that had been taken, I knew that my life was over too.

JD was all that I had. In 2009, I said that I would make him addicted to me. But God, I never thought, this "addiction" would be so painful and controlling. I am a prisoner.

I walked into the lobby to leave before the cop came back to my room. I tried to slip through a door on the opposite side of the lobby, so that JD wouldn't see me, but he did. He ran after me, and I couldn't run fast at all from all the pain I was in. When he caught up to me, he grabbed my arm, and we started walking down the street to find a taxi. *I'll never escape,* I thought!

Be anxious for nothing, but in everything by prayer and supplication,
with thanksgiving, let your requests be made known to God.
Philippians 4:6

21. Sherrell, July 2013

God, yessss you answered my prayers. Black is free to do whatever he wants, and he called me to let me know that he isn't in a relationship anymore. I am so siced. He asked me did I want to go bike riding with him today. This will be our first date. I told him yes, and that we can ride around Bowie. Black voiced that he wanted this "friendship" to be different so we agreed that we would not have sex right away. I was in shock. No one has ever presented that to me. I think I am falling in love with this man. He is like a breath of fresh air. However God, I am well aware that he just got out of a long-term relationship. My only issue is why would he pursue me if he needed time to heal? I question this about him, because he already said he wanted to wait before we had sex. So what is he doing? He's like a challenge. God, we had such a great time riding bikes today. I kind of introduced him to my mom and dad. It was very short and informal. To me, that was major. I never introduce any men to my family, unless I feel like they are going to be around for a long time. I don't know if Black knew how serious that was. The ride was so refreshing and hard at the same time. God, I thank you in advance for putting it on Black's heart to want to stop. When we finally did, I thought, *My legs are on fire, and I am really done. We've been riding for over two hours.*

Well would you look at this? God, you go so hard. It's a baseball field. I am so glad he asked me if I wanted to sit down and watch the game. Whew, my legs couldn't take anymore. God, this just feels so right. I cannot believe the way I feel about him. Why are my feelings so involved with him? God, could this be the man I have been praying for? God is he emotionally available? God, thank you for giving me a sign that he is the man I have been praying for. I can't even imagine what it looks like without him in my life. God, what the heck am I talking about? I am mentally moving fast, and I prayed for patience with him.

Okay God, my prayer is to cover him and show him where he needs to go. I know things in his life are crazy right now, and I don't want to add to that, so I thank you in advance for covering us both.
Amen.

Sherrell, November 10, 2013

Omgoodness Really God??? After four months of pure bliss with this man and he has the nerve to do this to me? I feel like we have been in a relationship for years. But obviously to him, I mean nothing. Things have been going so good besides that time he told me that he didn't want me to meet his son and his nephew. Okay, we got through that. I finally met them. But now after everything, God you mean to tell me that he STILL doesn't love me? What is this you have me in? I mean it's not like anything I have ever experienced. This screams love to me. He is so brutally honest. I finally get up the courage to express to him that I love him, and he looks me right in the eye and says, "I don't feel comfortable with you telling me you love me." God, I almost passed out. I could feel the room spinning and my heart in my pinky toes. Yes, God his words shrunk my heart. How could this be? We have made love, forced by me of course, and the way he makes love to me proves to me that he loves me. Everything about him is different. God, I ask you again, HOW COULD HE NOT LOVE ME? How does he feel like it's okay to tell me that he doesn't want me to say that? I am so confused, and I am giving up with this man. He is so honest to the point that it hurts.

Are these the qualities you have set for me? A man who can look me in the face and tell me to not tell him I love him, because it makes him uncomfortable? Is this a quality I have lacked in men my entire life? The ability for them to tell me the honest truth even if it hurts? Is this what I need? It hurts so bad to hear this. Somehow I have now fallen head over heels for him. God is this MY man? I refuse to continue this relationship knowing I feel so deeply about him and he doesn't want anything to do with me in that fashion. He is not ready to commit to me, and he is upfront about it. But God, I need him. He brings out the best in me. We have so much fun together. How could he not love me? God, I think he is running from the feeling of loving me. I can feel that he loves me. I have never felt that before. Why is he so emotionally unavailable to me? God, why are you making me wait? What is the lesson in this? God, I promise to try and slow my feelings for this man down, but I cannot promise that I can. My heart won't stop beating this whole album of music for him. I love him dearly, and I want him for me. God, I just want to know why are you making me wait? Amen.

He who hates, disguises it with his lips,
And lays up deceit within himself;
When he speaks kindly, do not believe him,
For there are seven abominations in his heart;
Though his hatred is covered by deceit,
His wickedness will be revealed before the assembly.
Whoever digs a pit will fall into it,
And he who rolls a stone will have it roll back on him.
Proverbs 26:21-28

22. Natasha, 2013

Lord, I am so miserable. But your word seems to comfort me. I have been seeing scripture from the book of Proverbs in my dreams. They are juxtaposed with my summer of terror, and the dreams turn into a daunting nightmare that I cannot escape. God, do you remember what happened in that house on Iverson Street? Did you see the fight we had on September 20th, when he beat me over and over in my face and ribs? Were you there as I was running down the steps, stumbling out of the house, and hiding in that bush for safety? I couldn't think of anyone to call to come and get me as I waited. When I get out of this Lord, I must start an organization to help domestic violence victims. One thing that's needed is safety transportation. I would have died that day, had I not found D's number in my phone. I sat there in that bush, and dialed my first boyfriend's number. The guy who taught me the game. He loved me so much, but I learned to love the fast life. I grew a love for music artists and drug dealers when I was thirteen! He was my high school sweetheart, and can you believe that he answered. He was just around the corner. OMG. As I think about it now, and I watch JD play that stupid game sitting next to me, I'm thinking about how real of a dude D always has been to me. Him and his man came and scooped me up immediately. *I know he would be pissed to know I was back with this loser.*

D didn't judge me. Instead, he took me to safety, God. He drove me all the way out to Calvert County to this amazing house in the middle of the woods. He had been renting it from one of his homie's, an older, divorced white hippie who had an alcohol problem. God, I couldn't believe it. D took me to the hospital in Calvert County. They told me that I had broken ribs, a fractured nose, a fractured finger, and my forehead needed attention. I can't believe how broken and damaged I was, still am, months later.

Lord, okay, so you're so funny. The day I left, JD went outside to meet the police to apparently file a restraining order against my mother. But she already had a warrant out on him, which he didn't know about, and he ended up getting locked up. I had sixty whole days away from him. You gave me a new computer, and you sent new clients my way. I had a new place to live, even if it is in this basement. Lord, why did I begin to see him and accept his phone calls and letters while he was in jail? Why did I write him back? WHY DID I LOOK BACK? Why did I accept his apologies? I read this bible verse the other day that really stuck with me. It was 1 Corinthians 10:13, *"No temptation has overtaken you except what is common to mankind. And God is faithful; he will not let you be tempted beyond what you can bear. But when you are tempted, he will also provide a way out so that you can endure it."*

God, I know that when he went to jail, and you provided me with a new place to live, you were giving me a "way out." Why didn't I just leave him alone? Why did I have to go back? I don't understand why I have this sick loyalty to him that I cannot break.

Natasha, December 2013

Wow! God you are so awesome!! I am so happy that JD and I moved! We live in this amazing top floor, two-story loft in Largo. It has a fireplace, cathedral ceilings, and a den upstairs. Oh and we have our own garage! You really showed out!! We were in that basement for exactly one year, but it seemed so much longer. I was listening to music, and something hit me that to get out of that slump and that we just needed to start looking for a place to live. Ever since we got out of there, I haven't had many nightmares about the summer of terror. We haven't had many issues, besides the stupid argument JD had with his baby mother's dude, when JD called him "Baby Tupac," lol. It seems like every few months, there is something petty going on with that situation.

Anyway, back to better issues… I realize that JD and I haven't gotten into any fights since he was released from jail in November of last year. It's been over a year! Okay, well, actually a few weeks ago on Thanksgiving, we did have an episode. But I take total blame for that. I was oddly in and out of sleep around 5a.m., and you know he wakes up early. So I thought I overheard him on the phone saying something to the nature of, *"When I call her, I just act like she's my sister, because I know her dude be all in her phone."* I FLIPPED! I jumped out of the bed, and I ran in the kitchen where he was and snatched the phone out of his hand and threw it at the wall and started beating him in his chest and I was screaming to the top of my lungs. I totally blacked out, and he choked me up, and banged me up against the wall so hard that I thought my internal organs were going to fly through my chest. That snapped me back into reality and woke me from any sleep that might have been lingering.

He denied it and told me that he was talking about his man's sister. I thought maybe I was trippin'. Maybe I was. Not sure, but he told me that he wanted *ME TO LEAVE HIS PLACE!* Can you believe him? Yes, the place is in his name, but I pay the damn rent! I can see now that this is going to be an issue. I have to get my name on this lease ASAP. I begged and pleaded with him all day to forgive me. I stayed at my friend's house, and the next morning he went out to buy a new phone.

Anyway, besides that one incident, things have be so perfect! His family has been at our house hanging out through the holidays. It's been so awesome to have some family back in our lives. I even saw Sherrella this week. She came by and we drank wine and talked like old times. She told me all about the new dude she's seeing, Black of Mumbo Sauce. I'm so excited that we both are in great relationships! Maybe you just wanted me and JD to stick it out through the wilderness.

Thank you God for answering my prayers!!

Promise me, O women of Jerusalem,
not to awaken love until the time is right.
Song of Solomon 8:4

23. Sherrell January, 2014

God, I haven't spoken with Black since November. I sent him a text message after we had a great weekend being snowed in and playing games, to tell him how much I loved him. It took him forever to respond, so I sent another text back saying disregard my text and to lose my number. When he finally replied, he was saying how he was in the shower, and that I was tripping after we had such a great weekend. I was pissed with him. We had been texting each other "ILY" for weeks now. What did he think I was saying? What did he mean when he texted it back? Either way God, why I am so obsessed with him? Why is he so guarded? God, I know he loves me, because I can feel it so strongly. But we have not spoken since then, and I miss him so much that it hurts. I keep posting subliminal messages on IG to show how hurt and angry I am that we are not talking, but he doesn't budge. He doesn't call or text. How can he be so cold God? Is he wondering the same about me? God, I pray that you place it on his heart to call me and to love me. I KNOW this is the man for me. I honestly think this is it. He brings me joy, and he even introduced me to his church last summer. Zion is the best church I have ever been too, but I haven't been because I am afraid I am going to run into him, and he won't talk to me. That would kill me. I miss church so much. That church was bringing me closer to you God. I know this is the enemy keeping me from church and keeping me from Black. Or are you keeping me from Black to take care of me? God, please continue to protect him. I know he has this new job, and I am so happy for him. I pray he is okay and not seeing anyone. I can't fathom the thought of him seeing someone or slipping back with his ex. God you know I don't want that to happen. God, I know this is INSANE, and correct me if I'm wrong, but I am starting to feel like I was created for this man.

Joe has been telling me to call him, because he is sick of seeing me look so miserable. He asked me today why am I fighting it so much? Joe has been a major help in my life, since we have been here. We complement each other and now that he sees JJ often. She and Gabby can play and build their cousin bond. We have helped each other as far as parenting, and also I have introduced him to Zion. I can hear him in the room reading the bible to my niece every morning. He is so committed to doing right by you now, God. But maybe I should listen to him and reach out to Black. Nope I can't. He may reject me, God. I want him to need me like I need him. Is that what it is? He's not like anyone in my past, but I want him to cater to me like some of them did. At least that way, I can know he loves me.

Wait, God what was that?? Did you just show me a sign telling me that this is not how it's going to go through this Lifetime movie? That was spooky, and on that note, I love you, God. Continue to stay with me. Amen.

*Give me not up to the will of my adversaries; for false witnesses have
risen against me, and they breathe out violence.*
Psalm 27:12

24. Natasha, January 4, 2014

I picked up this contract at an association, at the end of the year, making soooo much money! It's such a great gig, however I have to work in Arlington each day. I went back into the office on January 2nd, after being off for nearly two weeks during the holiday. I missed JD so much at work, so when I got home, all I wanted to do was hang with him and act like it was still Christmas time. We had such an amazing Christmas. But he told me he needed to go pay for his daughter's tutoring class, before the snowstorm came. At first I was going to stay home. But again, I was so pressed to be with him, and he also needed to get money out of my account, and so I decided to go.

Lord, I know I felt you telling me to just stay home. I have to learn how to be more obedient to your voice. Now my life is over.

We went to the bank to get the money.

He drove my car to Clinton, where his daughter's grandparents live.

I was writing tweets promoting my new book *The Build Up*, and he was listening to some of my promo.

We had Yo Gotti playing on the radio by the time we pulled up to the grandparents' house.

I saw his baby mother's car. Then I saw two dudes walking around the car, and I nodded to JD to make sure he saw them too. He got out to take the money order inside. I was still composing my tweet, trying to find the exact words to say.

He came out of the house about five minutes later. I loved watching him walk. He wore the black and red plaid jacket. I saw a tall dude step up to him, and ask him to step off and talk.

JD said he didn't know him.

"I'm Tupac, nigga!" said the tall dude.

That's when he swung.

JD stumbled, but he was also holding his hand to his neck or face.

I jumped out of the car.

I started screaming and yelling, asking the dude why he started a fight with JD's daughter in the house.

"Bitch, shut up before I stab you in the face."

The other guy choked me up and pulled me.

They started fighting, and I was trying to break away.

When I finally got away, and ran up to where they were to break it up, everyone fell to the ground.

The daughter came outside.

The grandparents came outside.

I saw the baby mother standing there too.

Everyone was yelling, and finally they broke it up.

JD got in the driver's side and tried to back out of the driveway.

I turned on the light once we got up the street, and I noticed the blood coming from his face and neck and everywhere else.

He looked weak.

I told him to pullover.

"You be my right, I'll be my left," he said.

I put him in the backseat, and he told me to hurry to the hospital. By the time we got there, blood was all over his head, face, and neck.

I went in and told the hospital workers we needed an ambulance. They pulled him out of the backseat and placed him in the wheelchair. I parked the car, then ran back to the ER and through the doors to find him.

He was on a stretcher, and they were cutting off his clothes. I kissed him on his forehead and told him he'd be okay. God, you know I immediately fell to my knees and started praying and asking you to save his life. *He couldn't die. I know I prayed for him, but why did you allow what happened next to happen to me? I'm so confused God. You know I'm not a bad person. Why am I in this mess?*

The more I talked to his mom on the phone, the more things were seeming a little off. I called her and told her what happened immediately, but when she called me back she said, "Natasha tell me the truth. Who stabbed my son?" Yes he had been stabbed nine times, God. Why? I told her the story again. She asked if I had a knife.

Then police came to question me over and over.

I told them the truth.

My truth didn't matter to them. They arrested me. I was confused.

How could you let this happen to me God? How could you let me go to jail for this? How could you let these people lie on me and frame me for attempted murder? How could I be facing so many charges, God? *I think my life is finally over. All those close calls with the law – are now like warning signs telling me to slow down and come to you, but I didn't it. I shouldn't have been so loyal to the point that my own life is now in danger.*

I need you now more than ever. I cannot believe that this is happening to me. My life has finally caught up to me, and now I don't know what to do. I truly want to kill myself.

Natasha, March 2014

The dude was charged with attempted murder. But they haven't dropped my charges yet, God. What's up? What's worst is that getting stabbed nine times and nearly dying didn't change JD. It only created an even worse monster. He keeps comparing himself to Jesus, saying that he's the only man besides Him that has ever risen from the dead. And if that wasn't enough, I found out he was cheating on me, or at least trying too. It's crazy that the weekend after he came from the hospital, I had his phone and this chick he used to deal with called. He acted weird when his phone rang and didn't answer, so I called her back from the phone when he wasn't looking, to see who it was. I immediately recognized her voice. He saw the look in my eyes and he knew what I had done. He flipped. He choked me out, and smooched me so hard my face hit the door. Then, the next week, he got mad because I now wanted to spend my 401k money that we had agreed to take out to invest in new businesses on a criminal attorney that will likely cost $10,000. Do you know he got mad, started a fight with me in the car, and almost ran the car off the road as I was driving? He told me to come in the house once we got back to the place, and I refused.

I went to Draya's instead. I came home around 3 a.m. and he had thrown all my clothes over our balcony. Then, I went in the house, and this chick is in there. She's not one of his hoes or anything. They're just friends, and this girl is also friends with Rella. She respects me, but it was the point that she was in *my house* at three in the morning, and I wasn't home. Oh and that day, I came home from work and he had spent my damn money on a flat screen television that cost nearly $600. Talk about LIVID! Lord, I'm so pissed I don't know what to do. How can I be fighting for my freedom and my life *after probably saving his life,* and he treat me so horribly?

Anyway. I know he's cheating on me with that chick, so I thought of a plan. At first, for about two weeks straight, I'd leave my laptop open on the desk in the den where he has the television, and it would be on all day recording his every move. But then I got scared, so I had to stop that. So I decided to go to Best Buy on Valentine's Day and buy myself a nice little gift - a mini recorder. And I knew the perfect place to put it. Every morning before work, that recorder goes inside of a book on my bookshelf, right next to the futon he likes to lay on. Yup. And when I get home from work, I listen to nine hours of recording to find out everything he did during the day. I am so exhausted trying to figure out his deceitful moves.

I needed proof and I got it. Today, I decided it was time to leave. He keeps fighting me, and it's getting really bad. The fights are worse than before. He's burned me on my back with an iron. He has bitten me and sent me the hospital at least twice this year, since he was stabbed. I cannot take it anymore. One day, he pulled my wig off and threw it over our balcony. Another day, he tried to throw me out of the car on the highway. The conversations that are on the recorder are disgusting and repugnant. I am so disgusted by who he is. I sleep with knives. I've been hitting up my exes trying to get my hands on a gun. They all know I'm crazy, and no one will give me one. Instead, they keep begging me to let them kill him. I can't possibly allow someone else to do my dirty work and go to jail for it. I'd rather do it myself, and it would be self- defense, since he keeps putting his hands on me.

God, I'm really afraid that I will end up in jail because of him. He tries to make up with me by having sex, and the crazy thing is, our sex is still good. It's sick. He asks me to marry him, and then he picks a fight with me. He has fought me in front of his female friends. Last week, I recorded a conversation of him making plans for one of his exes to come over to our house and have sex with him while I was at work. He sits on the phone all day, while I'm at work, calling girls to get them to come and have sex with him. What is his problem? Anyway, so once I got wind of that plan, I had him drop me off. Then around 10 or 11, I told my team that I was sick, and I caught the Metro and the bus back home, praying that I would catch him in the act. I came home too early. She wasn't there yet, and he left once he saw me.

This is crazy. I'm leaving today. My mom said one of her friends, a guy, would help us get my stuff out of that apartment. God, thank you that you did not allow my name to go on that lease. I know he won't let me go without a fight. This is going to be a WILD SCENE. God, please protect me. Thank you so much in advance.

Love is patient, love is kind. It does not envy, it does not boast, it is not proud. It does not dishonor others, it is not self-seeking, it is not easily angered, it keeps no record of wrongs. Love does not delight in evil but rejoices with the truth. It always protects, always trusts, always hopes, always perseveres.

1 Corinthians 13:4-7

25. Sherrell, April 2014

Thank you so much, God, for bringing Black and I together. It's been soooo long, and I missed him terribly. Thank you for making me get up to go to the Broccoli City Festival and do the workouts. He saw me there and called my phone. When I saw his number, I was a little irritated and siced that he was calling. I started not to answer until my ego knocked me to the ground, lmsao, so I answered.

"Hello," I answered like I was irritated.

"Look to your left," he said.

I looked to my left, and there he was on his bike outside of the gate at the Broccoli City Festival. On the inside, I had butterflies and was extremely nervous, but on the outside, I acted BOLD and like I didn't want to see him. He felt my tension, when I walked over to him. He made short talk, and I only gave him one word answers, and it killed me to be that mean for no reason. I am in love with this man. God why am I trying to act hard or not show him my true feelings? I really wanted to jump that fence and hug and kiss him so hard. I think the fear of rejection was haunting me. Black telling me not to tell him that I loved him was holding back my true emotions. I will never forget him telling me that. But God, seeing him ALWAYS gives me butterflies. Well he sensed that I was being a bitch, so he ended the conversation and said he would "holla at me." I was so sick. I couldn't even finish my workout.

I left the festival and I couldn't take it anymore. I called him and asked him if he wanted to go and get something to eat with me. He said yes. Thank you so much, God, for helping me to not be so gung ho on being mean to him and hiding my true feelings. I vow to try and stop being so guarded before I lose him.

Turn from evil and do good;
seek peace and pursue it.
Psalm 34:14

26. Natasha, 2014

I'm back at my mom's, and it's just like it was when I came back in 2012. She's snooping and judging me and trying to control me. I still have stuff at the place where JD and I lived and although I took him to court the other day for a restraining order, he called me right after and we talked. I am going to see him. I don't know why I can't leave him alone. I started going to domestic violence counseling. My therapist is truly making me understand this relationship for what it really is, and I feel like I'm finding myself again. I'm getting back to my old self. It's crazy, because during every fight that I had with JD God, I wasn't scared in those situations. I was more so scared of the cops and ending up in jail than I was of JD. Maybe that's you. Now that I am 90 percent out of that situation, I am actually afraid to ever have another fight with him. I'm afraid of what I may do.

For everyone who asks receives, and the one who seeks finds, and to the one who knocks it will be opened.
Matthew 7:8

27. Sherrell July 2, 2014

AHHHHHHHHHHHH OMGOODNESS!!! GOD, I LOVE YOU SO MUCH!!! BLACK TOLD ME HE IS ALL IN, AND THAT I AM OFFICIALLY HIS GIRLFRIEND!!!! I am the happiest girl in the world right now. He is my man, and I no longer have to wonder about us. I have always been very secretive about my relationships in fear that if I posted on social media, some girl could be messy or some guys would try to destroy me by bringing up my past. But GOD HE POSTED A PICTURE OF US ON INSTAGRAM!!!! It's real now. Just please stay with me and help me to not mess this up. The moment he said he was "ALL IN" my heart skipped a beat, and I just cried and yelled in the restaurant to everyone, "I'm his girl-friend now." They all clapped. God, I pray guidance over my boyfriend. I can't help but to smile from ear to ear when I say that. After all the breakups and silent days between us, we are now officially a couple. This is the day I have been waiting for. I love this man so much. God, please listen to him when he speaks, and let him know you hear him. I love him to pieces, and I want him to always be led by you. He is now the man in my life. Thank you, God. I couldn't be happier. Continue to stay with me.
Amen.

But the time is coming—indeed it's here now—when true worshipers will worship the Father in spirit and in truth. The Father is looking for those who will worship him that way.
John 4:23

"The Beautiful Struggle"

28. Natasha, August 25, 2014

The struggle of public transparency vs. public discretion.

The struggle of knowing who I want to be and what I want to do after building a life based on something I thought I wanted, but wasn't sure.

The struggle of having faith that it will all work out, when seeing no way out of (what might be) a box I am creating for myself.

The struggle of acceptance of myself, then acceptance from everyone else when I want to give two fucks about if everyone accepts me.

The struggle of confusion.

The struggle of believing in someone that no one else believes in.

The struggle of loving someone that no one wants me to love.

The struggle of knowing the truth, but believing a lie. Living a lie. Listening to a lie. That this is love.

The struggle of being a rebellious soul, captivated in a very closed society, of being a free spirit that won't fly.

The struggle of remaining silent to spare others' feelings, of listening to them underestimate me and allowing it. The struggle of feeling defeated when I constantly win, as they would say.

The struggle of spending day after day in my own head, unable to communicate what I feel to those outside of my brain.

The struggle of not being able to get close to anyone, to trust, to feel after I've been made numb.

The struggle of wanting to move forward, needing to move forward, yet being stuck in the past.

The struggle of not having anyone to talk to, to listen, to understand.

The struggle of seeing your dream deteriorate in front of your eyes and not having the strength, the understanding, and the wisdom to save it.

The struggle of fighting a losing battle, because maybe I'm fighting against God's will.

The struggle of being still, but restless.

The fear of accepting that I will not be my best.

The struggle of being an oxymoron.

Natasha, December 2014

God, these past ten months have been truly life changing. I cannot believe I have been through so much, and I am so in awe of how you delivered me. You showed me how my mouth, my bad temper, and need to feel a thrill (and feel love from men) have cost me so much and always put me in harm's way. Lord, you knew that my social anxiety was getting worse, and so even though I've been at JD's house a lot, because it's a comfort zone, God you placed it in my heart to join the social media ministry at church. Being able to serve you by sharing the word through the internet is changing my life. I am "at" every Sunday service and bible study, and I am getting stronger and stronger each day. I feel it's only a matter of time! A mirror has been held up to my face, and while I'm not in the public eye as much, you are still keeping me. It's amazing that I have so many amazing contracts with DC Government agencies, festivals, and non-profits. I am so undeserving of the success you give me in my business, but I thank you so much for it. I even had an opportunity to appear on Fox 5 Morning News to talk about the Arts & Humanities Festival. This has been a powerful year in business.

Okay, so God, I know that JD should have been out of my life by now, and he should also be a non-issue, but here I am still dealing with him. Thank you, Lord, for having those charges dropped and clearing my name. I don't know how you did that the day of my court case, but WOW! Thank you God for healing my heart of all the hate that I felt for all the people who betrayed me. I forgive them, and I know one day I'll forgive JD too. Thank you so much for prompting me to go to therapy, writing, and revealing all the blessings that came out of this past year. I wrote this book, and it's literally about ten months of my life, but it seems like forever. My sis and I have been trying to come up with the perfect name. Right now, it's called *The Re-BUILD*.

You know I love the word "build." And it's only right since Rella helped me rebuild and we came up with The Build Up together back in 2010. God, okay, so my issue now is that I have just gotten my biggest business contracts ever. We are also planning the Made In the DMV Conference, which is this weekend, and it's set to be EPIC. Everyone in the city is going to be there, plus execs from MTV, Revolt, and more. But I'm still living this double life. Although JD and I don't have a title, and we both have our own apartments (five minutes apart, granted), he's still been in my life a lot. I know he's not good for me. I just have to break this chain that I have with him. He brings out the crazy side of me that I've tried to overcome. A few times, I went to his house unannounced and caught him with the same ex-girlfriend. One time, I waited for hours, saw them pull up and go inside, and then I knocked on the door. He opened it and asked me not to start anything, that they were just going to smoke.

Well God, I promised you that I wasn't going to "start" anything, and so I said to him, "Why the fuck is this bitch here?"

I promise, I was not talking to or looking at her. I was talking to him *about her*.

From behind him, I heard her say, "You better get your girl, before I-."

Okay God, so that gave me a reason to go in. I said, "Bitch, shut up. I'm not talking to you."

She was closer to me now, and he was in the middle of us. She kept talking God and I flipped. I just hit her in the head, and we started fighting. But let's be clear. I didn't fight her because she was there. I fought her because she disrespected me. She ran out almost in tears, and I stayed and cursed him out.

It's been bad since then.

We crashed the cars in a crazy car chase a couple of months later. Afterwards, he punched me right in my mouth and now my tooth is chipped. His car is of course on my insurance. I refused to claim that crash. I got us both rental cars. We haven't really been talking too much for the past couple of weeks.

SMH. I can't believe as I was just writing tonight, he came to my door. I let him in, and I immediately knew he was drunk. I was actually working on my book. He came in telling me about how he had an amazing weekend with his fam—the NBA player whose party I got kicked out of five years ago. He then started to say something to the effect of, "Baby I love you. No girl can compare to you. But I realize that these girls love me. I can get anything from them. They will take care of us. So you should just be cool with that. You will always be my main bitch, and they can't compare to you."

I cut him off. I was furious that he was in my house trying to convince me to be his "main bitch." I have finally made up my mind that I WILL NOT go into another year with him in my life. I closed my computer and finally found the strength to say what I should have said years ago. And mean it.

"I'm done. You need to leave, because I realize that I am done with you."

At first he thought this was like all the other times and I was just talking. He asked me to stop joking, and after about five minutes of me saying things like, "I'm serious. I no longer want to deal with you. Get out. I'm over it. I've had enough. You can have all of those girls. You know my dream is to get married and have a family - that's my one dream - and you're trying to steal that from me."

Well God, he finally got it and he snapped. He started calling me all kinds of names. He then proceeded to pick up my flat screen television and take it out of the house. He accused my sister (who lives here) of stealing the television from his friend.

I tried to get the TV out of his hands. He dropped it and began to punch me repeatedly over and over in my face. Of course I was hitting him back. God, I don't want to make it seem like I don't fight back when he hits me, because I do.

Once he snapped out of it, he left. Then, I sat there in tears, wondering if I should call the police or go to the hospital. I drove myself to the hospital, sat in the parking lot for a very long time. I felt my face swelling. Then, I decided to go home and put ice on it. I have to make the swelling go down before the Made in the DMV Conference this weekend. I can't believe that I'm still going through this.

Why do I keep letting him back?

OH and P.S. - God thank you for allowing me to be honored with a PG County Forty Under 40 Award for 2015!! I feel like you're building me up to have an amazing year, despite this last bit of drama with my loser ex-boyfriend. I promise, this will be over soon, and I will make you proud of me.

Do two walk together
unless they have agreed to do so?
Amos 3:3

29. Sherrell, December 2014

Yessss God! This is a big day for me and Black. We completed the "Under the Hood" class at Zion, and today is the day we are accepted as official members of the church. How awesome is this opportunity? I am so happy to be doing this with the man I am totally in love with. He brings out the best in me and shows me every day that I am worth so much more than I give myself credit for. He is absolutely amazing, and I want to be his wife. Wow God what am I saying? I did say that I feel like I was created for him, and I still feel this way. I AM HIS RIB. It felt so good to accept the right hand of fellowship at the church today. My family was there cheering us on and of course crying. They are so supportive of our union, not just for me, but they love Black. They love that he brings out the best in me, and he loves Sherrell not Sherrella. My family never really accepted any of my previous men. They thought I was just settling because I didn't want to be alone. They were right. Black was different. He loved you, God, and wanted more of you. That is how I KNOW he HAS to be my husband. Lmsao. I may be getting ahead of myself, but God I am in love with this man so much. God, I just ask that you lead our steps and help us to continue to keep you first in our relationship.

Amen.

See, I am doing a new thing!
Now it springs up; do you not perceive it?
I am making a way in the wilderness
and streams in the wasteland.
Isaiah 43:19

30. Natasha, January 2015

Last DRAW! Two weeks before Christmas, I decided that I will not EVER answer another call or text from JD. He kept harassing me to get his car fixed from the accident. Although I probably should, since it was my fault, I'm not doing it. He's done me dirty, and there's no way. So anyway, at first he was calling me about that. I decided to go out to dinner with him again, and I immediately regretted it. He was so rude and loud to the waiter and was behaving like he has never been out of the damn hood. He's such a narcissist. I've been studying narcissism and narcissistic abusers, and he's all of that, God. Thank you for revealing this to me! I cannot stand him at all. I knew that night was IT! So I started to igg him. Then, he got this crazy idea in his head that I was sleeping with his homie, another artist from the city. I've been totally faithful to him. Even though we aren't even official anymore. So he proceeded to stalk me, show up at my house all times of day and night, and called me endless times. One day, I was coming home, and I noticed him following me. He parked across the complex, and as I was getting the bag of groceries and wine out of my car, he started to slow jog near my building. Then, he caught up with me on the stairs, and he noticed I had on a sweatshirt made by the guy he thinks I'm sleeping with. It was totally a coincidence. JD brought me the doggone sweater. He is nuts. I didn't understand it. He grabbed my groceries out of my hand and started throwing them all around the complex. He pushed me. But at that moment, I was not afraid of him. I said in my most stern voice, "DO NOT HIT ME." And then, guess what, God? He ran as if whatever demon that was possessing him fled. I ran in the house, and I VOWED TO NEVER EVER TALK TO HIM AGAIN EVER!

God, in that moment, I know I heard you say, "It's life or death." I know I heard your voice. I wonder if he heard it also. I haven't heard you speak to me like that ever before, and I'm terrified to test you on this. I had already decided that I wouldn't be taking him into the New Year. Your voice and his actions confirmed that. I just wish that the universe or Satan would obey your voice too. After that, he called my phone at least 100 times every day.

On New Year's Eve, after still not hearing from me for two weeks, he crashed his car into an elderly couple. Crazy! They are in the hospital. The police called and told me that I needed to come and get the police report for the insurance company. God, I just got my car back from the last accident. I do not want to report this accident. I do not plan on calling him either. I will have deal with the consequences of this accident that he caused, but I heard your voice, and you clearly said do not talk to him. So I'm not. I'm going to trust you. I know you're going to work it out God. This year, it's all about me and you. I promise this will be the best year of my life, and I will not let JD or anyone come between what you have for me. I know I am an amazing person. *You made me that way!* I love your word. I just want to be obedient to you, God. I WILL NOT LET HIM BACK IN! I'm convinced, he is Satan in the flesh, and most importantly, I am tired of doing crazy things. I just want a regular life. I want to serve you. I want to love you, and I don't want any more distractions. 2015 is MY YEAR!

Oh and P.S.- Thanks for making me go back to the book. We named it 10 Blessings of Betrayal, which I think it's going to be a HIT! I hear you prompting me to publish it next month on Valentine's Day. I can tell something amazing is going to happen when I do. Thank you in advance!

$\mathcal{N}$atasha, February 2015

God!! You rock! The week before the book came out, I went to church and Pastor Coates preached a message entitled "This is My Story. This is My Song." from 1 Samuel 2:1. I must share all the notes that I took. I was typing diligently, trying to catch every word of this, because I KNOW that this is your message to me!!

"THIS IS MY STORY, THIS IS MY SONG" - Delman Coates, PhD

Some Hip-hop artists use their voices as instruments to do what needs to be done.

Kendrick Lamar fuses his rhymes with hope and faith...

YOU HAVE TO HAVE A PERSONAL FAITH

Throughout the word of God, there are people who sing about adversaries, victory, and the steadfast love of God.

Today's text in 1 Samuel is Hannah's song of faith. We are given the theme about how God is able to turn the circumstances of life around.

God will intrude, intervene, and turn the circumstances of your life around.

There wasn't an adversary that Hannah encountered that was going to keep her from opening her mouth to sing to God.

You've to find a way to conjure up the faith to give God glory.

You'll be enabled to tap into singing in the midst of sorrow when you have a faith in God that is extremely personal.

You must have the ability to keep on praying and worshiping God in the midst of your trials. This is evidence of your faith.

The true measure of your faith is when you can praise Him when you are going through trials.

When you're going through a trial, it is not a time to sit home and hide from God. This is precisely the time when you need to be in God's presence.

YOU HAVE TO HAVE A PURPOSEFUL FAITH

In 1 Samuel, Hannah basically said, "God, if you'll bless me, I promise I will give this blessing back to you."

Don't pray for your sake, pray for God's sake... so that He gets the purpose of the blessings.

God has a plan and a purpose for your life that you can't even fathom or imagine.

When we pray, we ought to punctuate our prayers.

When you pray in Jesus' name, you have to punctuate.

When you go from praying a selfish prayer to a purposeful prayer, a door that was shut opens up. Have a purposeful prayer!

When you pray to God, you have to tell God that 'I'm going to put this blessing back in your hands.'

HAVE A FAITH THAT IS PRACTICAL.

In the text, after Hannah prayed for a child, she goes to church, then it says that her husband "knew her." (i.e., They went home and had sex).

Okay God! So I'm praying my Hannah prayer today!! The book comes out this weekend, and I promise that if you bless this project, I will give my blessings back to you. I will never look back again. I will honor your name and give you glory. I know that you wrote this book, and not me, and I know that people will be helped. Lord God, please don't let me totally ruin my career or my life by publishing this book. Please bless this and I will give *10 Blessings* back to you. I will teach people how to overcome their trials. I will lead people to you. I will worship you. I will not continue to disrespect myself or others. I'll commit to learning and teaching your word. I'll be your Communicator for Christ! In Jesus name, I pray, Amen!

OH P.S. - Thanks for prompting me to claim the car after all. I needed that come up! It's going to help me publish the book, and it's all for your glory. Thank you, Jesus!

Natasha, February 2015

Okay, God!! Thank you for answering my prayers!! That was SOOOO fast!! The book came out and sis gave me this genius marketing idea, and people are ordering it like hotcakes! I sold almost 200 copies the first week. I woke up one day to a text message from sis telling me that the book had made the Best Seller's and "Hot New Releases" selection on Amazon. I'm not quite sure what that means, but I'm here for it God! I just looked at my vision board, and it has the #3 besides the word "Books." That means I have to write at least three books this year. I have so much lost time to catch up on. I'm going hard! I finally finished and published *The Build Up Branding BluePRint*, and even though I didn't market it as much as *10 Blessings*, the people who have read it said they found it very valuable. God, you are so awesome. We had a private book release party for *10 Blessings* on Valentine's Day, and I read the book, and took a bunch of pics with so many of my friends and peeps that I'd been alienated from the entire time I was with JD. God, I've only been in this new life for two months, and I love it. I am not looking back again.

I filed a restraining order against JD last weekend, after he called and posted death threats before my book came out. Then the day of the release, he invaded my hashtag on Instagram with all this crazy stuff, and he even put out a sex tape that I didn't even know he had. God, I am not worried about him. He always hung my PR career over my head, and tried to control me by threatening to expose my bad past, but for the first time, I feel totally free. I do not fear what people will say about me. I don't care if he has

a sex tape. I am excited that I now have the evidence to take him to court and settle this matter with him for good. Thank you for being SO FAITHFUL TO ME!!! I know that you fight my battles now, so I will NOT fight anymore, not with him or anyone else! Praise God for deliverance.
#10BlessingsOfBetrayal #BestsellingAuthor #MamaIMadeIt. LOL. Okay, Goodnight God!

And let us not grow weary of doing good, for in due season we will reap,
if we do not give up.
Galatians 6:9

31. Sherrell, February 2015

God, please watch over my brother Joe. I don't know what's up with him. He keeps meeting all these random girls and the moment they find out we live together, they want to get him to move in with them or kick me out. I know my brother will never kick me out, but he ALWAYS starts a conversation like, "Will you want to take over this apartment if I leave?" Why would he even want to deal with these type of women? God, I pray for his flesh. We are so similar when it comes to this stuff. This time I think it's serious. He's getting serious with this one chick SMH. I'll keep my comments about her to myself. I told Black today that I have to get out of this apartment in two weeks. He now is trying to figure out how he can help. I asked him if he would be willing to move in with me here. He declined. He doesn't want this apartment to be our first place that we live in together and I totally feel him. I am running out of time and options. I know I cannot get an apartment with my credit. I could barely get a lollipop with the credit I have. I don't want to go back to my mother house. It's just not enough room there for me and Gabby. I may just have to make that call. However, Black has agreed to look for a place with me, a new place. So in the meantime, I will talk to my parents to make sure I can secure a place since our last day here is in four weeks.

God, since Black has decided to make these rushed decisions with me, we now have to pull our credit to see if we qualify for a place together.

Oh Lord, I am so nervous about this. God you know my credit is horrible and he has NONE. What are we going to do? We have applied to a number of different places only using Black, because we figured he'd have a better chance than me. And, God, no luck. Are you telling me that I should just stay with my parents? Please God, work this thing out.

Sherrell March 2015

OMGOODNESS GOD ARE YOU SERIOUS???? Black just checked his credit and the apartment he had on there is now GONE! God, I immediately started searching for apartments. I know this is you working, even though we shouldn't live together before marriage. This has to be a sign saying we are going to be okay. We pulled up to the apartment complex, walked in applied and now we wait.

Two days later…

We got the apartment. Thank you so much, God. Both of the kids have their own rooms. After months of viewing horrible apartments and also being turned down, we have the perfect place. It's not in the ideal neighborhood, but the great thing is that my good friend, who is an MUA, lives right downstairs. How ironic?!? Now it's time to tell the parents of our kids and everyone…But God you did this. Thank you so much! Continue to stay with us.

Amen.

And we know that all things work together for good to those who love
God, to those who are the called according to His purpose.
Romans 8:28

32. Natasha, April 2015

I can't believe my life!! After the book, I was featured in *Black En-*
terprise Magazine and so many other publications. I did my own PR… LOL
well, you did it for me! I feel like you worked everything out for my good,
God. Even though I didn't feel comfortable in the PR world back in the day,
you allowed me to excel, make great relationships, and meet so many people, because you knew the place where you were taking me. I can't believe
it!

Okay, so more great news, God. General Motors contacted me and
invited me to Las Vegas, to the Stellar Music Awards!! AHHHHH! I'm
screaming and doing happy dances. Then, one of my clients hit me up, and
asked me to start a women's group with her non-profit with my book. God,
what are you doing? Just a year ago God, I was fighting for my life in every
sense of the word. How is it that you completely flipped the switch on my
world so fast? I even met this amazing woman who my insurance agent told
me I needed to meet last year. This woman's name is Tressa, and she's a pub-
lisher and we're going out for coffee! I also met Mia Wright, another sur-
vivor, and some other amazing women, God. The people you have sent my
way are really blowing my mind. I cannot believe this. I also have a new
special friend. He's in the industry, but he's not like the others, God. We connect on a deep level. He's so protective of me, but in a sweet teddy bear way.
He gave me a book launch party and he's been so amazing. I think I'm falling

for him. But I don't think he can handle my dark past.

Thank you so much for delivering me, God. I love you and I honor you. I can't wait to start the women's group and begin pouring into them. They are going to know that through you ALL things are possible, and I'm PROOF!

Natasha, May 2015

Thank you, Jesus. This has been the most amazing trip to Chicago that I can remember. My dad's church invited me for a "book blessing." God, I was not sure what exactly a "book blessing" was, and I didn't expect to be treated so amazing. Well, his church just so happens to be a megachurch with probably well over 10,000 members. The pastor laid hands on me and prayed that *10 Blessings of Betrayal* would bless people around the world. After the service was over, they allowed me to take photos and sell the book, and at least 80 people waited in line to take photos and get my autographed book. I have shared over 100 copies while on this trip, and I cannot believe what you are doing in this season, Lord. But I just want to thank you. I truly don't deserve it. Aside from the church service, I've been able to see so many of my family members, and my grandpa. He's in a nursing home, but he looks so amazing! You know I gave him a copy of *10 Blessings* and he just smiled, and started reading. I love him and my dad so much. I thank God for my dad, because he was the one who gave me the advice to read Proverbs each day, while I was going through my mess last year. Just last year, I was reading the bible and praying for deliverance Lord, and now I see that your word never comes back void. Thank you.

Natasha, July 2015

God, you know how I feel about the 4th of July. I cannot. Take it. Every year since 2012, this holiday has been PURE HELL! I woke up this morning and decided to record an audiobook called *Fireworks* about becoming a victim of domestic violence on 4th of July. I pray this audio-book blesses someone! I recorded it once, with no script at all. It was so good that I pushed it out!! I'm so excited about this. I will not go to any cookouts. I don't want to be with anyone. I just need to let this day marinate, and serve you through my testimony, and I'll be HAPPY when tomorrow

comes! Thanks for keeping me and delivering me. I remember so many holidays spent by myself or miserable and alone with JD. I'm happy that, at least now, I have a choice of what to do on the holidays. Love you!!
Signed, Your Communicator for Christ

Natasha, October 2015

God! Okay, I have decided to never ever have sex again until you send me a husband. I found myself in crazy lust with this guy who seemed great for me on the outside, but he's such a jerk. We did it twice and it was toooo good. I'm afraid. I don't want to slip back into my old ways after doing so well. So I feel guilty. I'm so convicted. As soon as he left, I just fell on my knees and started crying. I think this is the point that you wanted me to get to all along. I get it now! My body is my temple. I will not have sex again. I will not be the old Natasha. I'm working for you now, and I REFUSE to risk that for LUST. I haven't listened to any secular music since February. I've been guarding my eyes and ears, because music makes me so vulnerable and susceptible to my emotions. I don't want to be that emotional wreck that I used to be. I listen to your word all day. I know everyone doesn't have to do this, but you know how I am. There's no gray. It's all or nothing.

I started taking bible classes at Evangel; these classes are amazing!! PAUSE: So I think I'm supposed to be a Christian counselor in a communications type way – like by writing more books and stuff. I absolutely love these groups that you have me doing, and I LOVE writing. And I took a Christian counseling class and was right in my element. I can perceive when others are hurting and how to comfort them through your word. God, maybe I had to live the life that I did in the past so that I can accomplish what you put me here for. I know I am called to help the broken hearted.

I thank you even for that last bout of depression in July, because it pushed me and sis to start our new business, B&D Brand. I have been speaking a lot on Periscope, and we already have over six clients and our schedules are packed with discovery sessions all day. It's so funny how as soon as I started living for you, everything began to make sense. I wish I knew that this was the key to being happy the entire time. Another amazing thing that happened is that I've been linking with all these domestic violence survivors, and so we decided to begin a coalition to help 10,000 people break free. It's going to be called 10 Blessings 10K Survivors. *Ha! You know that though.* Our photo shoot was today, and we ROCKED IT!! I'm so happy. I can't risk my future by returning to my past ways. Nope. I repent. Please forgive me for having sex, and you can mark my words, I will be obedient in that area from now on.

God, you are so funny!! I wrote three books on that vision board, and I've already released three books of my own and I've gotten four ghost-writing clients since I published my book, and guess what!! They are ministers, Christian Coaches, AND...... drumroll please!! That amazing woman Tressa linked me with THE Dr. DeeDee Freeman of Spirit of Faith Christian Center, and I met with her and her daughter Brelyn today. Brelyn's wedding to gospel singer Tim Bowman, Jr. went VIRAL because they were both virgins and she presented her father, a famous preacher, with a purity certificate at their wedding. The world is going crazy over this wedding. And how is it LORD that you've found me worthy to help her with her book? Crazy!! How did this happen the same week that I decided to stop having sex until marriage? LOL. #iCantWithYouGod. Nobody would believe my life if I tried to explain these things to them, but I know you're just speaking to me through my work.

Romans 8:28 is at it again, I see! I'm looking forward to learning more about Brelyn's views on purity and honoring you. This is going to be very, *very* interesting!

Don't you realize that your body is the temple of the Holy Spirit, who lives in you and was given to you by God? You do not belong to yourself, for God bought you with a high price. So you must honor God with your body.
1 Corinthians 6:19-20

33. Sherrell, August 2015

God, after months of attending church, I told Black that almost every time we leave church, I feel so conflicted. The sermon is not even about sex, but I feel like Pastor Battle and Pastor Marshall are always speaking directly to us about blocking our blessings by not being obedient. I have missed what I thought would be the opportunity of a lifetime to serve as lead on the health and wellness ministry because we live together. I am so upset, God. I know the church is right, but they don't realize how valuable I could be to the church. I expressed to Black that we are blocking our blessing by living together and not being married. He doesn't feel as conflicted as I do, God. However, he does wish he could hear you and feel the Holy Spirit as I do. What he doesn't understand is that this comes from all the pain and mess I have experienced. I have opened myself up to you. I just pray that he finds it in his heart to understand that we need to honor you first in all that we do. I am an entrepreneur and he is an artist and entrepreneur. In order for our lives to be blessed abundantly at this point, I think we have to take sex out of the equation. He is about to go on a two to three month tour. I pray you renew his mind and start to prepare his heart for this stage in our lives.

Sherrell, October 2015

I knew that you could answer our prayers whenever you wanted to God. Why do you make me wait so long for certain things and others you bless me with right away? Lmsao. I will never understand the delivery of my blessings. SMH. I will just continue to pray and make sure I do everything in my power to stay obedient.

Black called and asked me what I thought about practicing abstinence at the beginning of the year and taking the premarital class at church when he got back. God, this man just proposed to me. I was silent on the phone for about 30 seconds. I screamed "YESSSSSSSS I DO" LMSAO. I'm sure he didn't know that I was saying "yes" to marrying him. I took that as his proposal. I couldn't have been happier, God. All I could think about was fighting for him to love me openly and not fight it and now he is asking me to marry him. I couldn't wait for him to get home so I could see him and talk to him about everything. God, thank you so much for staying with us! Amen.

For God has not given us a spirit of fear, but of power and of love and of a sound mind.
2 Timothy 1:7

34. Natasha, November 2015

GOD I NEED YOU NOW!
I think he's trying to abduct me.
I think he's running a sex trafficking ring.

Dear Lord, help me. I know I was slippin' tonight, and I let my guard down. I can't believe I'm in an unfamiliar country, by myself, with no way to reach my mother. I am pretty sure all of these women in here are in this country against their will. I am trying to think of a way out of this situation. I need to get out of this dark office. I heard everyone else leave, and I believe I'm by myself. *Why did I treat Shelton so mean, God? Yes he was coming on strong, but honestly, now that I'm thinking back—who cares? He wouldn't have hurt me. At least I know something about him, but this guy, I know nothing about. Curiosity killed the cat!!* OMG. Why did I have to be so curious about this mysterious man? You know my desire is to honor you COMPLETELY, and now I am scared to death that he is going to rape me. I don't feel fear often God, but right now I am scared. Please help me. I thought my attraction to *his type* had subsided. I thought I had been cured of poor decision-making with men. *MY goodness, it was the drinks. I should not have mixed drinks.* My judgement is all off, and now I'm in a jam. God, please grant me the grace to make it through this. I thought I grew up, Lord. God this cannot be the end of what you designed to the most amazing year of my life. *Okay, Natasha, think. BIBLE.* What does YOUR word say? *"For I know the plans I have for you declares the LORD, plans to prosper you and not to harm you, to give you hope and a FUTURE!"* That's it! Hope and a future.

Your plan is to prosper me. I'll keep repeating that to myself. That is my word. *He will keep in perfect peace, all those whose mind stays on Him.* Okay, God. My mind will stay on you. I will continue to talk to you. I will continue to pray to you. *Plans to prosper you and not to harm you.* God, I know that even if this man intends to harm me, you will not allow any weapon formed against me to prosper! That's it. I'll keep repeating these words. This man cannot hurt me, because your word is my shield. I am speaking it. He cannot hurt me. No weapon formed shall prosper. Okay here he comes, God. This cannot be the end of me. Okay, Lord. I have learned my lesson. Please keep me safe through this one last jam. God, I promise no more slip-ups. I know that I cannot do things on my own and give into my flesh not for one second. God, I have learned my lesson. I promise. If you get me out of this Lord, I will never make this mistake again. I will never allow alcohol and lust to cloud my judgement. God, what do I do? Tell me what to say!

Earlier tonight:

It's my last night of vacation: I want to leave the resort with this guy, Shelton. He's much older, and he's not just any guy. My mom knows his friend and we are all sitting at the bar. I don't like him, and I'm pretty sure he knows that, but he's being sweet… like an uncle or something. So maybe he'll show me around town. I want to get away and go experience regular life with the natives…

First Shelton and I went to a bar that wasn't poppin' at all. We had a drink and left. Then, we went to the casino. It was boring, so we left after a little while, and then he took me to this strip club. This is where the night got interesting. As we were walking in, I immediately felt Shelton get closer to me. He tried to grab my hand and hold it as we were walking through the doors of the club, but I acted like I didn't see him.

At the bar:

He keeps trying to hold me, kiss me, and act like we're a couple. I think he's intimidated, because the club owner keeps eyeing me. The minute I laid eyes on the owner of the club, I was turned on by him though. He looked like he was from the States. I knew we had some things in common. He's a hustler for sure. I could definitely tell that. He learned that I like margaritas, and he keeps giving me drinks. I need space away from Shelton, so I am going over by the stage to talk with the dancers. Being here is taking me back to all the nights I partied at The Stadium. Except, something is not quite right with these girls. Some of them are very talented, and others look really 'green.' They also all look like they're from different countries… Costa Rica, maybe Kenya, Jamaica, Guatemala, and the list goes on. *Maybe I'm just trippin.'* They're all very exotic, but not that sexy. Some look like they've had extremely hard lives.

I immediately started sparking up conversations with them, to learn more about what brought them here. Okay, God. So Shelton spotted me, and he came and sat next to me in the front of the stage and he keeps giving me money to tip the strippers. I know his type, and I don't like it, God. Does he think I am going to get drunk and turned on by these girls and then go home with him? He has it mistaken! He is definitely taking me back to my hotel. So I just need you now. I dipped away from him again. I made an excuse to go to the bathroom. But instead, I went upstairs, because I saw the club owner sitting in this remote spot in the cut watching his business from a balcony. I quickly found the nearest staircase, and kept watching the stage to make sure Shelton didn't see me creep off upstairs. I go and sit next to him, and he said, "I was hoping you'd come up here."

"Really?" I said.

"Yeah. Tell me about yourself."

He and I talked for about 20 minutes, as we watched the girls go on and off the stage. He told me he was originally from New York, but he had to leave, because it was getting "hot." He said he had some charges and served some time, but was let out on a technicality. He was supposed to go back to prison, but instead he moved out of the country, and he's back and forth from here to Costa Rica. I asked him about the club and everything seemed normal. He then told me he had to go back downstairs to close up.

"I wish that I could talk to you for a little while longer," he said, and as he was leaving he said something to the effect of *"You'd fit in really well here."* I believe that comment slipped by me, because I was still wishing he could stay upstairs and continue the conversation. I'm not sure what it is about bad guys that I like. I'm living for you now God, and as soon as I spot a guy who is similar to all the guys in my past, I fall. Why? Anyway, I told him that I was blown because I came with someone else. Come to find out, he and Shelton know each other well. *Still*, this is my last night. I'm not ready to go back to the hotel, and I don't want to leave with Shelton, because he's creeping me out. I must quickly devise a plan to get my flip flops and t-shirt out of his car, so that I have no excuse to see him again. I'd also need a ride home, although I'm sure the owner of the club will take me home.

As I was caught in my thoughts, he stood up to leave, and I followed his lead. We agreed to chat later, and I went back to the bar where Shelton was eagerly awaiting my arrival. I sipped my drink and went to the restroom, and when I walked out, a security guard was standing at the door waiting for me.

"Mr. Newman would like you to meet him upstairs."

Wow, I thought.

I liked "Mr. Newman."

He was a G for sure. I followed the security guard up a windy back staircase in the cut of this hole-in-the-wall club, and I was upstairs in Mr. Newman's office. My eyes immediately gravitated toward the white stripper pole coming out of the small circular white stage in the middle of the floor. *He must have a lot of "private meetings" up here,* I thought. I put that thought in the back of my head, and continued to follow the security guard to a room. He opened the door and there were several screens monitoring everything that was going on in the club, outside of the door, the dancers' dressing room, the bar, and the cash register. Mr. Newman was inside counting his money.

"What's up, beautiful? So are you going to hang out with me for a while? I know Shelton isn't your type, so I thought I'd rescue you. I'll take you back to your hotel so you can hang out a little while longer and see the city if you want."

Hmm… okay, but I have to be back before 4.

"That's cool. Let me finish up here, and we can leave."

Mr. Newman got up and went outside of the room. I watched him on the cameras as he went to another place in the club, off cameras. I immediately felt this heaviness fall upon me, and it felt like fear. *Maybe it was your Spirit, Lord.*

Then I went outside of the room, because I was starting to feel creeped out in that dark office surrounded by all of the cameras.

As I was leaning over a rail next to the stripper pole, I feel a presence behind me. It was Shelton. *OMG. Quick. Think Natasha.*

"Oh, so you leave me and come up here with this dude? You do not know what you're getting yourself into, Natasha. I will protect you. Come now."

Then, he grabbed my arm. I yanked away from him. By this time, I was feeling the tequila from the six or so margaritas, and I was also pissed that he was trying to control me.

"Oh, you want to stay with him? Is that what you're doing? I took you out, and showed you a good time, and now you want to ditch me for him?"

Immediately, I felt HORRIBLE. But regardless of my feelings, the drinks were controlling me, and I did not want to leave with Shelton. I said,

"Let's go outside so that I can get my things out of your car. I appreciate you showing me around, but I don't feel comfortable with you, and I'd rather catch another ride home."

He gave me the most hateful look that I've seen in a while and stared at me in disgust. "Fine, but you don't know what you're getting into. You are being a stupid American!"

So that was it. I started walking down the spiral stairs, down the hall, and out the door. I marched to where he had parked his car, as he followed behind yelling at me. When we got outside and the cold hit my face, I snapped back to my senses. I turned to him, and said,

"Can you take me back to my hotel please? You're right. I don't want to stay. Please take me back now."

"No. You cannot get in my car. I will not take you back."

"WHAT DO YOU MEAN YOU WON'T TAKE ME BACK? YOU WERE JUST BITCHING ABOUT HOW I WAS BEING A STUPID AMERICAN. Fine. Give me my things and I'll get a ride back."

I sat there, as he refused to open the door. When he finally did, he reached inside, threw my flip flops and a t-shirt at me, and I walked away in my 4-inch heels, feet screaming waiting to get out of those things.

He then did the most *annoying* thing ever, and he began to drive beside me, and started shouting obscenities to me through his Caribbean accent. I was PISSED and embarrassed that he was drawing attention to me in front of the crowd of guys that had now formed outside of the club. It was the "let out." I pushed passed the guys, and through the doors. When I came to the second door, I met the security guard who had escorted me earlier. He gave me a nod and moved out of the way so that I could get back through.

The club was empty now. I could hear Mr. Newman arguing with a female upstairs, and I stood at the bottom of the stairs so that I could over-hear and wouldn't interrupt.

She was speaking in another language, but she was going back and forth to whatever her language was and English. I heard her say something like, "*What is that bitch doing here? What are you doing? Don't do this.*" He was yelling back at her, and he told her to mind her business and go "to the house."

She stormed out. That should have been my cue to leave, but I was weighing my options. My phone wasn't working properly. It was 2 a.m. My ride had left. I knew no one else. I walked out to the bar, and I saw a young guy that I had noticed working behind the bar earlier. "Can I see your phone?" I asked him. He shook his head "no" and walked away.

DEAR LORD. WHAT IS GOING ON?

I had no choice but to go back upstairs. When I did, I was met by

Mr. Newman, who immediately pulled me close to him and began speaking to me in a very low voice. His lips were very close to mine, and he said in a very calm manner.

"You aren't ready to go back yet are you?"

"Um, soon," I told him.

"Well it's not time to go yet." He then sat down and began to tell me how he and his brother had to make a trip out of the country to the DR to pick up some girls.

I asked, "What do you do?"

"I buy women. My brother sells weight in the States but it was getting too hot. So I figured out another game. I moved here, and found this spot. It's really a sweet deal, because the girls want out of their countries, because they aren't making money there. All I have to do is promise them a place to live and $400 or so a week."

"So you mean, you are prostituting women?"

"NO. They dance here. Or they may clean or do whatever else I need to do. I mean some of them entertain tourists. They each have a place to stay, and they're not complaining. Stop asking so many questions. Are you the police or something?"

Lord Jesus! My questions always get me in trouble. I need a way out of this fast. He told me to follow him to the dark room. My heart was beating fast. As he spoke, I saw this dark shadow become a cloud over him. I felt fear. I knew immediately that he is what the bible would call a wolf in sheep's clothing.

Submit yourselves, then, to God. Resist the devil, and he will flee from you.
James 4:7

35. Sherrell, January 2016

Okay God, we need you so much right now. We are starting to practice abstinence and it's a snow storm and the kids are not here. This is a true test. What are we supposed to do? All we can think about is sex. Our first couple of days practicing abstinence and all I can think about is having sex with my man. We bought a lot of games and stuff, but for obvious reasons, God, I cannot stop thinking about making love to him. Just please stay with us and let us make it through this patch. Is it going to be this hard all the time? Is it really that bad to have sex before marriage? Why, God, now do I want to ask these questions when we decide to do this, but it's so hard and it's only our third day. But how could you put us in this position? LMSAO. This is just unfair. We'll continue to stay in our corners. Is masturbating in front of each other acceptable?

…

Okay, I guess not. I'll just keep cooking, and he will continue to find movies. This is so hard already. Please stay with us.
Amen.

Then Jesus laid his hands on his eyes again; and he opened his eyes, his sight was restored, and he saw everything clearly.
Mark 8:25

36. Natasha, January 2016

My grandfather died so I spent my New Year's riding from Maryland to Chicago, during a bad winter storm, with my cousin and his dog. Dear Lord, he is so sad because he and Grandpa were best friends, and I am not sure what to say to him. I cannot believe that Grandpa is gone. My dad preached his eulogy, and I learned that my dad would go to Grandpa's job in the summers when he was growing up. Every day my Grandpa would read Proverbs. Since there are 31 of them, he would read whichever Proverb corresponded to the calendar date. I know you were speaking to me in that service. That tradition that my grandfather started was passed down to me to help me come out of my darkest hours. I thank you so much for that. I also thank you for all of my amazing family, cousins, uncles, great uncles, and family. I learned that we have a ton of preachers in my family on my dad's side. One of the Browns in Georgia is a doctor, and when his wife learned who I was, she grabbed me by the hand and told me I had to meet her husband. They learned of my book, and God you won't believe this. The doctor-preacher was also wrongfully accused. He talked to me so long about how amazing you are and how there is something great in store for me. He encouraged me to keep sharing your word through my work, and I will. I thank you for Grandpa's life and all of the new family that I've met. So often, when I was little, I felt like a step child. But this trip showed me that I have always been your daughter and my earthly father, grandfather, aunts, and cousins love me too. Thank you for allowing me to see these things.

Keep your heart with all vigilance, for from it flow the springs of life.
Proverbs 4:23

37. Sherrell, March 2016

God, I am so nervous. This is our first day of premarital class, and it has been three months since we have been practicing abstinence. We have had some really close calls but, because of prayer, we have stuck it out. This process is mentally painful. It is causing me nightmares and mental breakdowns. It's almost like I can feel the soul ties leaving me daily. I have caused so much spiritual friction to my body, and now it's time to give it all back to you. I am so willing to do whatever I have to do to have this man as my husband forever. He wants this extravagant wedding. God, I just want to go to the justice of the peace. I don't care about having friends and family there. The only two people I desire is my dad to give me away and my Granny to be alive to see this. Granny has been a MAJOR staple in my life. She is the closest thing to Jesus to us. She has prayed over me many nights after I left the club and did something INSANE with God knows who. God she never judged me. She only went slam into prayer. Granny is my everything, and since losing Grandma, my mother's mom last year, who was one of best friends in life, I value Granny that much more. So Black knows where I stand with this whole wedding thing. We are super excited about taking this step, and we cannot wait to start the class. God please stay with us in our minds and in our hearts.

Amen.

Do not be conformed to this world, but be transformed by the renewal of your mind, that by testing you may discern what is the will of God, what is good and acceptable and perfect.
Romans 12:12

38. Natasha, June 2016

Riding back from North Carolina with my 10 Blessings 10K Survivors sister, Tokeitha, and her little sister. God this weekend was so transformational. I am so blessed for this experience. Several of us spoke at the It's Already Better Women's Conference in Raleigh. There were probably about 200 women there, and God I thank you for giving me that word to speak and confidence to preach the way that I did on how to move from "Tragedy to Strategy." I know the Holy Spirit filled me as I spoke, because those words and that passion could not come from me alone. Today we went to New R.O.C.C. Church and had an amazing worship experience. Afterwards, Bishop Ellis spoke to me Lord, and I know it was a word from you. I've been so conflicted about whether or not to stay at Mt. Ennon and on the Social Media Ministry, which helped me get through my toughest times, or to move to Spirit of Faith Christian Center with Pastors Mike and DeeDee. God, ever since I worked with them on their books, I feel like my life changed. My faith has increased, and now I understand your word and your will for me more. I spoke at Dr. DeeDee's conference, and at least a thousand women were there. I met so many people who said that my testimony helped them. I'm so thankful for these opportunities to share my testimony. And Pastors Mike and DeeDee were sent to me by you. You knew that I needed to get ahold of certain lessons about patience, your promise for me, purity, and my faith. They pour into me so much, and I feel like you are moving me into ministry. I love them, and I love how they have created the environments for success for their entire family. I see them as role models and the word that Bishop Ellis spoke to me gave me confirmation. I am going to become a partner of Spirit of Faith. I am also going to pursue your word. Yesterday, I did not speak Lord, you preached through me. It felt amazing to connect with you and people that way. I've been looking into attending seminary online at Liberty University for a while, but something just isn't right. I'm just going to keep praying and keep moving where you guide me. My first move is my new church. I'm going to call Dr. DeeDee right now and tell her the news! I'm going to ask her to put me to work.

Thank you Lord for answering my prayers. In Jesus' name,

Amen.

Let us hold fast the confession of our hope without wavering, for he who promised is faithful.
Hebrews 10:23

39. Sherrell, July 2016

Omgoodness we are finally finished premarital class. What a long 12 weeks, but so fun and EXTREMELY informative. We have taken things from this class that I don't even think Pastor Marshall knows were seeds he placed in us. We have had extensive 4-5 hour conversations God after each class. We have rated each other on characteristics and so many more exercises. This has truly been hard and necessary. God, I know I have been extremely impatient when it comes to my future with this man, but is it time? Will he ask me to marry him this weekend? This is the weekend of our two-year anniversary. I pray that he uses this time to propose to me. I am REALLY becoming impatient with just being his girlfriend. God, please show him that I am ready. Or am I?

He didn't propose. What is he waiting for God? I have told him over and over again that I don't care about a ring or a damn wedding. I told him that I would marry him in our bed with morning breath. I just want to give him everything. I want to honor you and only you. I want you to get the glory in this union. Show him that I am ready, God. Show him that I need him and only him. Show him that he is my husband. Though I know he knows, show him I am ready to be his wife. I need him, God. I am seeing more and more of you in him. I also think his prayers about needing more of you have been answered. I just pray that before my birthday this man marries me, and let's get to really building life together. I just pray that whatever your will is that it is done.

> *Call to Me and I will answer you, and I will tell you great and mighty*
> *things, which you do not know.'*
> **Jeremiah 33:34**

40. Natasha, July 2016

Okay, you are AMAZING!! I have never EVER felt your presence like I did today. I cannot believe this. As I drive back from Virginia Beach, I feel like a giddy little girl. I had to get on Periscope and share the news about how excited I am about this. I clearly heard you speak to me today while I was on that campus. Although I can do this degree online, I KNOW WITH ALL OF MY HEART that you are calling me to Regent. I am going to move there! I am going to pursue this degree in divinity, and I am going to be active in this Christian community. I am so excited that you gave me this revelation. THANK YOU JESUS! I was so scared when things started to get shaky with the business in May and I had to move, but now it all makes sense. You were weeding things out. You were making room for new. Lord, you know this has been such a time of discomfort. I've been feeling like maybe I did something wrong to end up in the wilderness again, but NOPE. Today, I clearly heard you. Virginia Beach is my new home. I need to begin making plans, because I am NOT LOOKING BACK! Please bless this process of me being admitted into seminary, finding a place to live, and getting my business back stable so that I will have the finances to do all of these things. I love you so much, and I have ABSOLUTELY NO DOUBT that these things are already done.
In Jesus' name, Amen.

Trust in the Lord with all your heart, and do not lean on your own understanding. In all your ways acknowledge him, and he will make straight your paths.
Proverbs 3:5-6

41. Sherrell, September 2016

God, I ask that you PLEASE help me. I have not had the energy to work out. I have been so depressed all month. I can't eat. I can't sleep. What the hell is going on with me? I have gained so much weight. I have been drinking during the day. Finances are so low. What is happening? Am I falling into depression? God, please SNATCH me out of this slump. Why am I depressed? Or am I really depressed? What is happening? Is the enemy working on me? I rebuke that spirit in the name of Jesus. I want my HUS-BAND! I know that's what it is. Why hasn't he married me yet? It has been 10 months, and I am FED UP with being his girlfriend. I am done with it. This is becoming so redundant, and I am not for sitting around for this mess. God, doesn't he know I love him with EVERY fiber in me? Doesn't he know I would give all of me to him? Am I being ridiculous for needing this to happen? We have been to a billion weddings this year, and I am sick of it. I don't want to go to another wedding. I am so over it. He keeps asking me about what I desire in a wedding. WTF is wrong with him? I told him it makes me uncomfortable to talk about it. I mean really God? Question after question about a damn wedding, and he hasn't officially proposed to me. So irritating. Last month while we were eating crabs, I told him it makes me uncomfortable for him to call me his fiancé. So this mf'er gets on his knees with crabs all his hands and pulls a Martin. He said, "Sherrell Diane Woodward, will you marry me, damn?" I was furious. I didn't respond for two minutes. I am so done with all this. No I'm not, but I am tired of waiting and it is TRULY depressing me. Is it because I have no control of when it is going to happen? God PLEASE SHOW HIM THAT I AM READY, PLEASE!

This last week of September has been so annoying and depressing. I haven't eaten and my breath tells the story. I have had the hungry breath all week. Why is this last week so hard for me? God, I know you are doing NEW things. You have to be. I feel like I am dying. Black is acting so funny. My mother doesn't want to talk to me. My clients are cancelling their appointments. My father won't even look at me when I visit them. I just need October 1st to get here NOW. Why does this feel like a detox? It doesn't feel good at all. I feel like pure S.H.I.T. I am sorry God, but I feel terrible. Please let this month just be over.

*To the weak I became as weak, that I might win the weak. I have become
all things to all men, that I might by all means save some.*
1 Corinthians 9:22

42. Natasha, September 28, 2016

God, I've been having a hard time getting up out of my bed. I am here now in VA and I started school. I thank you for making your plans for my life come to pass, but Lord sometimes I feel so tired and lazy, and out of place. I sometimes don't think I belong here. I really cannot believe that a girl like me is in seminary. I thought that your promise for me to come here was also contingent upon me getting a job here so that my school would be paid for…. Well, I thank you for the job God, but why did I have to be so embarrassed in the process. I got the offer, got the start date, and then, my background check came back. I found out I had a warrant from missing a court date. *Only ME!* So anyway, I went and turned myself in the weekend before I started seminary.

While I was so blown to be walking back into that jail to turn myself in, I am glad that I prayed the way I did. I prayed for you to use me, God, and that's exactly what you did. I cannot believe I was sitting there in jail all night ministering to the girls who came in my cell. I just pray that you bless Shante, Lord. She is facing some serious crimes. She's being charged with killing her babies, and she has no bond at all. God, I pray that you keep her, and that she draws near to you. I asked her if she knew you, and she said she knows that you exist. I asked her if she'd ever accepted the Lord as her savior and she said no. So I said the prayer with her God. I believe that is why you sent me there, and you allowed me to go through the embarrassing process of applying for that job. (Pause: I cannot believe I actually applied for a 9-5. I cannot imagine going back to work in a regular setting after almost 7 years as an entrepreneur). Anyway God, I will do anything for you

127

and to get closer to your word. I thank you for sending me to that jail cell with all of those women. I pray that my words stay with them, and they stay in faith, God. Please strengthen them. Please let them know that through YOU they can do all things. God, please protect Shante in there. I told her to cry her eyes out while she was with us in the temporary holding cell, but when she got transferred she needed to put on her big girl panties. God, I hope she doesn't tell everyone the crazy story she told us, because it sounded like she may be insane and she may have in fact killed her babies. Lord, I'm sorry. It's not my place to judge. Please just protect her. While I was in the cell with her and the others, I kept hearing the devil teasing me saying, "You can't make a difference here. *I thought you were a Tragedy to Strategy Coach. I thought you were a Communicator for Christ. But look. These women don't want God."* Lord, I know that was a lie, and I know that you came into that prison to save souls and you are going to continue to work on everyone there. I spoke your word to the correction officers, and I even shared some revelation about the process (since I know it so well, SMH) to a younger guy who was waiting to see the commissioner with me. Thank you, Lord, for your word and your wisdom in that situation, and thank you for teaching me one final lesson, TO GET MY 'ISH IN ORDER before I left.

Today, after I finally pulled myself out of bed. I wrote this sticky note that says, "You are on assignment for <u>God.</u> He needs you. Get Up!" I put it beside my bed, so that it would encourage me to get up each morning. Then I looked on Facebook, and saw that Sherrella has been having a rough month. I texted her a few words of encouragement, and she told me she's been also feeling really lazy and depressed (*WELCOME TO THE CLUB, I THOUGHT. THE ENEMY IS ON THE JOB*). I sent her a picture of the note I wrote and she gave me a Rella response and started praising you. Right now, God, I am asking that you keep her, Lord. Sustain her, encourage her and strengthen her. She doesn't realize that in a matter of days, she will be a wife, and what she's going through now is only temporary. It's her last test before the testimony. Thank you, God for keeping her. I love you so much, and I'll be praying for her this weekend. I cannot wait to see her walk down the aisle. She is going to go BALLISTIC once she realizes what Black has been planning. God, thank you for giving this to her, Lord. Thank you, thank you, thank you for connecting Black and Rella. After everything she's been through, I am so excited that she will get her happily ever after. And, we're so much alike God. We've done so much together and to see that you've chosen her for this gives me hope as well. I believe that one day I'll find a love as beautiful as Rella and Black's. I thank you now for that Lord and I claim in done in Jesus' name!

But for now God, can you please just keep my friend from going crazy over the next three days? Keep her encouraged, Lord. She does not know that her WHOLE LIFE is about to change BIG TIME! Yesssss!

For all the promises of God in Him are Yes, and in Him Amen, to the glory of God through us.
2 Corinthians 1:20

43. Sherrell, October 1, 2016

OMGOODNESS I AM A WIFE!!!! THANK YOU SO MUCH GOD for staying with my husband and pouring into him!!! God, he had been planning this day for months and I had no clue. I apologized to him for being so mean and making him feel terrible because of my attitude. I am the happiest girl in the world now. You answered my prayers and his too. You are so amazing! I am so proud of my husband. God, when I walked into my own surprise wedding, I could feel you all in there. God, I can tell you this because I know you will understand. But when I reached my husband (Wow, MY HUSBAND) I felt like I can see YOU and not him. I saw your power running all through him. Wow, that is so powerful. You are so BAWSE!!! I cannot believe he was able to keep this HUGE secret from me for months and the people involved also. Today was filled with anxiety, but I am so elated at your power and your timing! All I have been praying for is for him to love me and make US official and today he did just that in a MAJOR way, JUST WOW!!! God, I kept saying you were doing new things and, MY GOD, you are! Thank you for ALWAYS staying with us and making this day so GRAND!

Thank you for saving my life and staying with me forever. Thank you for sending this man to me. Thanks for making me wait! Thank you for making me BOLD and EXTRAORDINARY!!! I LOVE YOU WITH MY WHOLE HEART FOREVER!!! Now let me go do as you say in your word and make love to my husband with NO LIMITS!!!
Amen.

130

Part 3
WRITE.
Through Daily Devotion, Write your Prayers and Confessions to God

Day 1
Acceptance

"Before I formed you in the womb I knew you, before you were born I set you apart; I appointed you as a prophet to the nations."
Jeremiah 1:5

The world we live in today is so judgmental. It creates this illusion to make women feel like we have to be perfect. We have to wear our hair a certain way. We have to smoke and drink to be cool. We have to have a certain body type to be attractive. We have to sleep with men if they buy us dinner. We have to have sex in order for a man to "like" us. God wants us to have relationships with people that give us life and that are created from love, not materialistic things.

The feeling of being unappreciated and not wanted is very painful and can cause mental trauma. Sometimes people can go above and beyond to feel accepted and they miss their blessing that God has for them. No one person is greater than the other. God is BAWSE and that is it. He created us to be perfect the way we are. He enables us to grow daily and that is the only way to our perfect. It is not the acceptance of others, but only of Him. God is looking for you to consult with Him about your imperfections versus consulting with the world. Don't miss your blessing, chasing the likes of someone else. Once you know and understand that God accepts you, you will feel a brand new confidence that when people don't accept you, they do not belong.

Pray:

Dear Lord, I thank you for making me unique in every way. I am not as confident in these areas above, and I need you to help me see myself the way you see me, God. Your word says that you knew me before I was formed in my mother's womb, which means you created me exactly the way I should be. Please restore me to the ideal version of ME that you have designed, and provide me with complete confidence and assurance that I don't need to be accepted by others, since I am accepted by you.
In Jesus' name,
Amen.

Day 1
Write: ——————————

What is it about yourself that you feel you just HAVE to change in order for someone to like/love you? List those things and ask God to reveal what HE thinks about those items.

_____

_____

_____

_____

_____

_____

_____

_____

_____

_____

_____

_____

_____

_____

_____

_____

_____

_____

_____

_____

Day 2
Confession

Therefore confess your sins to each other and pray for each other so that you may be healed. The prayer of a righteous person is powerful and effective.
James 5:16

Everyone has a past, but the trick of the enemy is to make *you feel* that your past is *so bad* that you should be ashamed and keep your secrets buried within your memory and your mind. If the enemy can be successful in causing you shame, making you afraid of your truth, or in fear of the consequences of sharing your past, he can truly manipulate your mind and keep you living in a world of darkness. Light and darkness cannot occupy the same space. Jesus is the way and the light, and the word tells us to confess our sins to other Christians and pray to receive healing. This promise from God is so freeing, because it literally closes an open door that the enemy has been using to keep us in fear, shame, and dwelling in darkness.

Darkness cannot dwell in the light. Begin to face your past and confess issues haunting you to someone that you trust, or perhaps a counselor, friend, or even to God in the form of journals or prayers. When you do that, you will experience peace. It will feel like a huge load has been lifted. There is freedom in confession. For years, Natasha's past had haunted her, and when she decided to publish her first book, she did so to free herself from the bondage of darkness and to be obedient to God. Since that moment, she has lived life free of the shame that her past caused her. You can experience that same freedom. Today, begin to recall the moments in your past that have caused you shame, hurt, embarrassment, and pain.

Pray:
Dear Lord, I am not perfect. You know this! I've made so many mistakes in my past, but right now, I confess my sins to you, and I ask for complete forgiveness and relief from the shame they have caused me. I denounce any works of the enemy to attempt to silence me into shame. I am no longer controlled by the world of darkness. Lord, today I come asking you to reveal to me a Christian sister or brother who I can trust, that would be willing to

pray with me and listen to the troubles of my heart. Thank you, God. I love you and I honor you. In Jesus' name,
Amen.

Day 2
Write:

What experiences have you been ashamed to confess to other Christians or to God? Write them out.

_____

_____

_____

_____

_____

_____

_____

_____

_____

_____

_____

_____

_____

_____

_____

_____

_____

_____

_____

_____

Day 3
Self-Control

"Think clearly and exercise self-control. Look forward to the gracious salvation that will come to you when Jesus Christ is revealed to the world."
I Peter 1:13

Being free to say whatever we feel to people that may upset, hurt, or treat us badly is ALWAYS easiest, right? The pressure to hold back can be so overwhelming and unnecessary when you feel betrayed. To have the power in our tongue to verbally abuse someone feels great at the time. It also shows that we are at the mercy of our temptation and we are being controlled by them. Can you imagine it? The thought alone is scary. By not controlling ourselves, some of us deal with life-changing temptations that can hurt us for a very long time. So why in the world would we let those same bad habits control our destiny? We do not have to be controlled by our desires, generational curses, or our strongholds. Those things make you feel weak. But I have news for you, God made us powerful and strong enough to fight off those bad habits. We just have to practice our strength and have control over our temptation. Work hard on not arguing with that girl on social media who always leaves bad comments or the guy in Starbucks who always gives you your coffee at room temperature. They are not worth you giving into your temptation. God has a better plan for the outcome of your day than to be angry and boast about how you cursed someone out on social media. Trust in Him and resist your temptation. Take charge of your life and break free from bad habits.

Pray:
Lord, I come to you today thankful for your ability to transform me to be more like Jesus. I ask for the grace that I need to practice self-control over any and all areas that are not pleasing to you. Please transform my character, my attitude, my thoughts, and my environment so that I constantly abide in your presence. I surrender all to you and I thank you for working in and through me. In Jesus' name,
Amen.

Day 3
Write:

What areas of your life do you need the most self-control over and why?
Remember this is not something that will happen overnight. However,
taking the time to recognize it is the first step to overcoming these issues.

_____

_____

_____

_____

_____

_____

_____

_____

_____

_____

_____

_____

_____

_____

_____

_____

_____

Day 4
Patience

Be joyful in hope, patient in affliction, faithful in prayer.
Romans 12:12

Have you ever been promised something that you had to wait for? Seems like the hardest thing to do, right? Truth is patience and is not optional. The moment that you try and rush God's process is the moment you miss the final destination of your blessing. Every day in our society, we see that patience is fading away. Everyone is rushing for something: love, marriage, kids, riches, jobs, etc. But the fact is that we have no control over when God decides to bless us with the desires of our heart and the abundance that he has for us.

Though the countdown seems like a million years, patience demonstrates your faith in God. It exemplifies that you trust God's will and His promise to you. Going through the process of waiting is when God is working His miracles to make sure you receive exactly what He has for you, and that you are ready for it when it does arrive. Just wait on God, and trust His process for your blessings.

Pray:
God, I trust in you and I thank you for strengthening me during this process of waiting. I will work diligently each day to submit and live in obedience, so that I am ready to thrive in your purpose in my life and with every blessing when they arrive. In Jesus' name, Amen.

Day 4
Write:

Think of all the things you are waiting for. Write them down and ask God to reveal to you if these are the things he has for you.

_____

_____

_____

_____

_____

_____

_____

_____

_____

_____

_____

_____

_____

_____

_____

_____

_____

_____

Day 5
Purity

Teach me more about you; How you work and how you move, so that I can walk onward in your truth, until everything within me brings honor to your name.
Psalm 86:11

We've all heard the saying that "sex sells." Television, entertainment, and social media networks constantly force feed us oversexualized images of women to sell everything. This saying has become popular to brainwash our society into becoming comfortable with talking about sexual relationships, seeing sexual images of women, and consuming sex in songs and on television. When we are indulging in all of this SEX the world feeds us, so we often don't stop to think about the fact that everything we consume has a negative or positive impact on our hearts. We cannot erase what we see, however, we can control what we choose to do with it. Sexual purity is not popular and to MOST it is corny and you are considered a loser if you have not or are not having sex. Truth is once you have sex, you are emotionally and mentally tied to that person whether you want to be or not. People think that they can immediately lose feelings or interest in a person they have sex with. As much as we'd like to believe that, it's not true. You saw the damaging effects sex had on the lives of the authors. Many times, we as women walk around depressed one minute, angry another, and anxious the next. We have so many different emotional ties pulling at our heartstrings from all the past sexual partners that we become bi-polar and unsteady versus stable and secure.

You have given A LOT of you to a sexual partner and you don't even realize the confusion you have caused with your own heart. There are a lot of women who refer to themselves as "Man Eaters" because they "feel" they can have sex and be done with that man. Well, that's not true. The heart will never forget, and it causes great pain and confusion which may show up in another area of your life. Think about some of the people, music, and places you are involved in and ask yourself, "Do these things promote what God wants for me?" Fighting against those things can be overwhelming and may seem unnecessary, but it is a requirement in order to honor God.

God loves us so much and wants to protect us from all things evil, especially the ones wrapped up in pretty bows, diamonds, and exotic vacations. Most people run to the things that seem cool and accepting in society, but they are evil and sinful. But society glorifies these things. Can you imagine how diligently God is working on the perfect man who He has already set apart for you? Shouldn't you allow him to do that same work in you so that you will be equally prepared for one another? This someone will be the person to live your dreams and share all of you with. God is and has done that for us. We have to practice patience and PRAY for peace over our flesh so that no temptation can control our destiny. If it is your desire to honor God and receive your blessings, then purity until marriage is a requirement of the kingdom.

God wants you to be in total submission to Him, and He wants your heart and mind to be clear so that He can use you for work within His kingdom. We cannot truly do God's work to our fullest capacity if we are consumed, heartbroken, or prioritizing things that are not of God.

FYI: Purity does not **just** mean abstaining from sex either. Realize that pornography, masturbation, and other sexual and lustful actions and thoughts affect our hearts and souls as well. In addition, marriage does not fix sexual impurity issues. So if you're a lustful and sinful thinker or participate in sinful behavior before marriage, it will only get worse afterwards.

Pray:
Heavenly father, I submit my mind, body, heart and emotions to you. Please make me pure and give me the strength and self-control to withhold any temptation. In Jesus' name, Amen.

Additional Verses to Strengthen your Purity Journey:
Create in me a clean heart, O God, and renew a right spirit within me.
- Psalm 51:10
But put on the Lord Jesus Christ, and make no provision for the flesh, to gratify its desires. - **Romans 13:14**
Therefore, if anyone cleanses himself from what is dishonorable, he will be a vessel for honorable use, set apart as holy, useful to the master of the house, ready for every good work. - **2 Timothy 2:21**
Do not be unequally yoked with unbelievers. For what partnership has righteousness with lawlessness? Or what fellowship has light with darkness? -
2 Corinthians 6:14

Day 5
Write:

What are some boundaries you may have to set to keep your heart and flesh pure?

_____

_____

_____

_____

_____

_____

_____

_____

_____

_____

_____

_____

_____

_____

_____

_____

_____

Day 6
Fear

The LORD is my light and my salvation— whom shall I fear? The LORD is the stronghold of my life— of whom shall I be afraid?
Psalm 27:1

Fear is the feeling or emotion that something or someone is dangerous and may hurt you. However, in Hebrews 13:5, God states that, "I will never leave nor forsake you." This is the truest statement of all time. Whether you believe it or not, God is ALWAYS with you, even in your mess. The thing is you MUST believe this statement to be true and practice your faith by praying, reading your bible, and fearing NOTHING but God.

Things like this are always easier said than done, especially when our minds are NOT made up. Have you ever heard the saying, "Faith without works is dead?" Well it's true. You have to work on your faith every day in order for it to prove active in your life. You have one thing to prove daily to God, and that is that you trust HIM and only Him wholeheartedly. Pray every day and ask God to deliver you from your fears. Ask Him to cast the demon away that is haunting you. God works MIRACLES. It may not be on your time, but He always makes a way for you to be pulled from your mess. God loves hard and will bless you with an abundance of miracles if you trust Him with your fears and give them all to Him.

Pray:
Lord, today I release all of my fears to you. I know that you will protect me God, and that no weapons formed against me shall prosper. Lord, I fear only you and I pray that you continue to build my confidence in you, your word, and that I will overcome any trials that may come my way. Thank you for your love, grace, and protection. In Jesus' name, Amen.

Day 6
Write:

What are you afraid of? Do you trust God enough to list them and let it go TODAY?

Day 7
Boundaries ─────────────────────

The law of the Lord is perfect, converting the soul;
The testimony of the Lord is sure, making wise the simple;
The statutes of the Lord are right, rejoicing the heart;
The commandment of the Lord is pure, enlightening the eyes;
The fear of the Lord is clean, enduring forever;
The judgments of the Lord are true and righteous altogether.
More to be desired are they than gold,
Yea, than much fine gold;
Sweeter also than honey and the honeycomb.
Moreover by them Your servant is warned,
And in keeping them there is great reward.
Psalm 19:7-11

The Lord is perfect and His way for us is perfect. God sets specific boundaries that we are to live within. Often, the enemy gets into our minds or the minds of people close to us, and he makes us feel like the boundaries in our lives are unfair or unnecessary. Just think back at what happened with Eve in the Garden of Eden. God had given her and Adam permission to eat fruit from all the trees except one. Satan came and deceived her, and made her believe that she was missing out on something, because she couldn't have fruit from that one tree. In reality, God had set a healthy boundary to protect them, and He knew what would happen should she cross that boundary. We have to remind ourselves and others in our lives that the same is true for us. Boundaries are healthy and they are set in place to protect us.

We are made in the image of God, and we are to imitate Him. Therefore, it is only right for us to establish boundaries for the people and relationships in our lives. So many women feel obligated to others. Maybe you feel obligated to take care of people, show up to every event, answer calls at all times of night, accept client appointments whenever *they are free,* or participate in sexual or immoral activities to please someone close to you. If you do not set boundaries for how you will spend your time and resources, people will run you ragged, and you will be used up until you have nothing to give. So many of us handle family and relationship obligations—we are dance moms, football moms, we volunteer on several committees and ministries, and we constantly show up for all of our friends and family members in need. While there is nothing wrong with giving of yourself and your time, you must set time aside for yourself, and realize that boundaries are healthy for everyone. When you set a schedule, that includes time by yourself, with God, volunteering, exercising, and spending time with family, and some time to do absolutely nothing, you will find yourself less stressed and more willing to help others in need. You will also experience a level of peace that you may be missing now.

Pray:

God, please release me from the lies that I have to do everything for everyone and give of myself until I have nothing left to give. Please speak to me and share the way you want me to schedule my time and allocate my resources. If there is anyone who does not belong or who constantly disrespects my boundaries, please change their hearts or remove them from my life. I pray that all my time, resources, and relationships honor you. In Jesus' name, Amen.

Day 7
Write: ⎯⎯⎯⎯⎯⎯⎯⎯⎯⎯⎯⎯⎯⎯⎯⎯

What areas in your life are unbalanced and could use boundaries? Are you ready to create boundaries in those areas today? If so, list them, and then begin to allocate your time and resources. You may need to use a calendar on your phone to plan "me time," "friend time," "boo time," etc. If you have any unhealthy relationships with people who are constantly pushing or overstepping boundaries, list the names of those people now.

GOD MADE ME WAIT!

Day 8
Love

Know therefore that the Lord your God is God; he is the faithful God, keeping his covenant of love to a thousand generations of those who love him and keep his commandments.
Deuteronomy 7:9

It is with great pleasure to let you know that God's love is unconditional. That may be hard to understand due to the way we know love and experience love with other people. Often loving another fleshly being can be hard because they don't live up to our expectations, and we unconsciously put God in that same category. However, God never rejects loving us no matter what we do. His love is unfailing and timeless. It is the kind of love we all yearn for when we need it most. But God loves us unconditionally on a daily basis. His love never leaves us. You are God's share of his chosen people. He designed you before your mother knew about you. He is so faithful to the ones he loves, and that's YOU!

The best part about God's love is that there are no strings attached. His promise was to love us unconditionally even in our mess, and He is the only spirit you can rely on when it comes to promises. In order to experience God fully, you must give your life to Him, show Him how much His love means by praying, reading His word, and worshipping Him in His holy name. When you get you some of Jesus, your life won't be the same. The things that used to matter of the world won't matter anymore. Love God unconditionally, and, then and only then, will you will feel what "love" is really all about.

Pray:
Dear Lord, thank you for loving me. Your love is enough for me, and I ask that you only send people that would love me from your lens Lord. Please work on my heart so that I might become more loving towards others and demonstrate your grace through my daily interactions. In Jesus' name I pray, Amen.

Day 8

Write: ═══════════════════════════════════════

Thank God today for loving you in a way that is immeasurable. Thank Him daily. Write it down on a Post-it note, business card, your money, anywhere. Remind yourself of His love wherever you go.

_____

_____

_____

_____

_____

_____

_____

_____

_____

_____

_____

_____

_____

_____

_____

_____

_____

_____

_____

Day 9
Drama

As for a person who stirs up division, after warning him once and then twice, have nothing more to do with him.
Titus 3:10

Some people are toxic - period. As a woman of Christ, it's important for you to have no tolerance whatsoever for people who threaten God's position, plan, and purpose for your life. This doesn't mean that you must cut off those who are closest to you completely, but establish boundaries to keep drama out of your life. This is so important, because drama disrupts peace and gets us off track. The best way to eliminate drama is to allow the word of God to transform your own thought life and behavior. Then you will develop a natural indicator that can sense drama. You will become naturally disgusted by it too. Your brain will trigger a red flag, and you can cut it off before it totally penetrates your spirit. The next time someone calls you with gossip, complaints, negativity, or faithlessness, cut it off and dismiss yourself from the conversation, OR, use that opportunity to speak life and pray for the person. The bible says in James 4:7, that if you resist the devil he will flee from you. Do not give any attention to the demon of drama.

You have probably experienced drama of some sort in the past. Maybe you have a girlfriend, sibling, lover, or child who is constantly bringing drama your way. Drama is a distraction that the enemy sends our way to get our minds off the business of God and onto issues of darkness. Have you ever thought about how much time and energy that it takes to entertain drama? Now imagine using that energy on something that God would like you to focus on. When you keep drama away, you have more focus and become mission-driven, versus drama driven.

Pray:
Dear Heavenly Father, I want peace. Please remove all sources of drama from my life. Bring to my mind any situation where I may be tolerating, welcoming, or causing drama in the lives of myself and others. I thank you for restoring me and I ask for your grace to transform me into a woman of COMPLETE Godly character. In Jesus' name I pray, Amen.

Day 9
Write: ————————————————

List the people, relationships, or situations that tend to suck you into drama. Next, identify what prompts the drama or why you have become a magnet to those things. There is an open gateway that welcomes drama in this area of your life. Once you discover it, you can close the entrance for good. On paper, think through ways to remedy those situations.

_____

_____

_____

_____

_____

_____

_____

_____

_____

_____

_____

_____

_____

_____

_____

_____

_____

_____

_____

Day 10
Peace

Submit to God and be at peace with him; in this way prosperity will come to you.
Job 22:21

It is the most beautiful thing to know that God wants us to have supernatural peace. Can you imagine that after having a stressful day at work, dealing with crazy coworkers, homework with the kids, bill collectors calling—after all this God wants you to have peace? This is the kind of peace that will have you smiling at your hectic day and thanking Him for getting you through. God will give you peace in all areas of your life if you let Him.

Resting is a form of peace. It restores your mind, body, soul, and spirit. Your body needs that restoration in order to operate at your greatest capacity. Rest prevents frustration and quick tempers. The body cannot be at peace if you are exhausted. You are on edge, and any and everybody will get a lash of it. That is not what God wants for us. Instead, all we have to do is admit and acknowledge that we need His peace. Then, we must slow down and meet God with our new found peace.

You can have peace anywhere and for any amount of time. You can always abide in God's presence with His everlasting peace. If you need peace of mind or rest in your body, try simple activities such as sitting on your balcony, taking a deep breath at work in your office, praying in your car. Get what God has for you. Guard the peace that God gives you with all that you have.

Pray:
Lord, you are the Prince of Peace, and I thank you for promising me that same peace. I commit all of my worries and cares to you, and I acknowledge that I need your ultimate and complete peace in my life. Please guard my eye gates, my ear gates, and my heart from any and every thing that threatens my peace in you. Thank you, Lord. I believe that these things are already done. In Jesus' name I pray, Amen.

Day 10
Write: ───────────────────────

When do you feel like you are most peaceful? Are there things in your life that prevent you from having the peace God gave you? Write them down, and commit those things to God as you write.

_____

_____

_____

_____

_____

_____

_____

_____

_____

_____

_____

_____

_____

_____

_____

_____

_____

_____

Day 11
Purpose

Whether, then, you eat or drink or whatever you do, do all to the glory of God.
I Corinthians 10:31

Far too often we cling to titles and hold dear to them because we feel like they validate our existence. We do all these things without consulting with God. We have high expectations of the things we are doing and if they fall apart, we immediately feel worthless and begin a pity party. All of these things are happening withOUT GOD. We begin to get depressed and feel insignificant like we don't matter. We look at inspirational quotes and apply them to our failed situation. These are all made up analyses in our heads. We let people categorize us if we don't live up to their expectations. It's understandable.

However, if we live for God, then we are exactly where we are supposed to be... unless we have been running from God and doing things that he did not ordain for us. (If you fall into the latter category, repent now and ask God to guide you toward purpose). So many people are confused about their purpose and are not sure if they are doing what they are "supposed to be" doing in life. Here's the litmus test: Have you submitted to God and are you being obedient to Him?

You must realize that purpose is a special invitation from God for you to participate in His mission for the world. Purpose is so important that when you finally begin walking in it, you will be contributing to the Kingdom of God. Why in the world would God waste something so important on someone who is not ready to receive it? How can you be living in God's ultimate purpose for your life if you are not even living for God?

If it is on your heart to be a singer and that is what God has for you, than be the best singer you can be. *However,* you must first dedicate your life to God and be obedient to His will so that He reveals *His purpose* for your life. Remember that we were not created simply to populate the earth and enjoy life. No, we were created because God had a specific plan for our lives that would contribute to *His* ultimate plan in bringing mankind in close fellowship with Him.

So if you feel like you are living in your purpose and that purpose is only serving you, and not honoring God and helping people, we have some sad news for you: That is not your purpose, dear. We all have a purpose that cannot be measured by the world's standards or taken away by people in the world. There is no scavenger hunt to know your purpose, God's got you. Live for Him and all will be revealed.

Pray:

Dear Lord, I submit my complete life to you. I know that my life is not my own, rather, I am here to work on your behalf and accomplish your mission for my life. Dear Lord, please reveal my purpose to me, and please send me the people and resources that I need to thrive in that purpose. I also ask that you remove all things that do not fit with your purpose for my life. In Jesus' name, Amen.

Day 11
Write:———————————————————

Are you constantly measuring your life according to what others are doing, in order to find your purpose? If so, STOP NOW. That is not what God wants for you. You are working backwards. Your life is so valuable and God needs you to know that. Your purpose is directly related to talents that you have and gifts placed in you by the Holy Spirit (see Romans 12). What are you good at? What people do you like to serve? What gives you joy? What problems do you want to solve in the world? Write them down.

_____

_____

_____

_____

_____

_____

_____

_____

_____

_____

_____

_____

_____

Day 12
Testimony

And many of the Samaritans of that city believed in Him because of the word of the woman who testified, "He told me all that I ever did."
John 4:39

When we share our testimony about how God has brought us out of a life of sin, and into the light, we encourage other believers. We give people hope that they too can be redeemed through Jesus. Our speech is so powerful. God created the world by speaking it into existence. So if you use that same equation, imagine the world you can create for yourself or others by speaking your truth. Of course there is a time and place for everything, but when God says speak, SPEAK. Revelations 12:11 tells us, *"And they overcame him by the blood of the Lamb and by the word of their testimony..."* Not only does sharing your testimony benefit you, but it helps others triumph Satan and be freed from the strongholds he has over them. Stories save souls, so just imagine what could happen when you begin to speak out and testify to the amazing things God has done and is doing in your life. Do not be afraid to honor God through your everyday conversations, social media posts, and interactions in your professional life. Become a #Communicator-ForChrist and watch how God uses you as a mouthpiece for the kingdom!

Pray:

Dear Lord, please use me to be your communicator and a mouthpiece for your Kingdom so that I can encourage others through my words and testimony. Lord, I ask that you speak through me and tell me exactly who needs a word of encouragement and when. Please place on my heart those who I can help, through my testimony. In Jesus' name, Amen.

Day 12
Write:

What can you testify about today? How has God blessed you this week, and how can you share this good news with others?

_____

_____

_____

_____

_____

_____

_____

_____

_____

_____

_____

_____

_____

_____

_____

_____

_____

_____
_____
_____
_____
_____
_____
_____
_____
_____
_____
_____
_____
_____
_____
_____
_____
_____
_____
_____
_____
_____
_____
_____

Day 13
Favor

For the LORD God is a sun and shield; The LORD gives grace and glory; No good thing does He withhold from those who walk uprightly.
Psalm 19:7-11

Favor is not fair. People sometimes ask, "How did they get that?" or "Why do they receive so much attention?" Some may wonder why everything you touch is successful, or how come you get the best clients, have the most amazing opportunities, or the most romantic spouse. What God has for you is for you, and that statement is true for all of us. His word says that "No good thing does He withhold from those who walk uprightly." Therefore, your job is to walk and live your life for Him and allow Him to do the rest.

Too often, people miss their own blessings and overlook the favor on their own lives because they are too busy watching someone else's. The 10th Commandment says, "Thou shall not covet." That means that you should not desire something that is forbidden (because it belongs to someone else).

Instead, if you recognize someone that you admire, then perhaps you begin to learn what they did to receive it or become who they are. There is nothing wrong with having role models or mentors, but we should not have idols and we should not expect or want to have a blessing in exactly the manner that another person has it. The favor that is on your life as a child of God is totally unique from anyone else's and God is so BAWSE in how he's custom-made favor, blessings, and abundance for each individual child of His. He is a great Father and as a child of His, you will experience uncanny favor.

Pray:
Father, today I come to show gratitude and thanks for the favor on my life. I thank you for protecting me, honoring your promises to me, and withholding no good thing from me, simply because I am your child. God, please forgive me for the covetous, jealous, or unappreciative behavior that I have displayed in the past. I thank you for making me exactly who I am and for making me more than enough for this world. I come to you in gratitude and

love, and with a heart of humility. Thank you for blessing me and my family and for keeping your hand on our lives. In Jesus' name, Amen.

Day 13
Write:

Convey your gratitude for the favor on your life. What blessings have been custom-made for you, and how does it make you feel that He has selected you for those blessings and favor?

_____

_____

_____

_____

_____

_____

_____

_____

_____

_____

_____

_____

_____

_____

_____

_____

Sherrell Duncan & Natasha T. Brown

Day 14
Temptation

No temptation has overtaken you except such as is common to man; but God is faithful, who will not allow you to be tempted beyond what you are able, but with the temptation will also make the way of escape, that you may be able to bear it.
1 Corinthians 10:13

We are tempted each day, and before the word of God lives in our hearts, it is easy to believe that we have no options or power over our own temptation. It's easy to feel like we must give in to the temptations of sex, the need for power, to portray ourselves as something we're not, to control others, idolize money or material possessions, lie, cheat, steal, gossip, drink, drug, or sulk in our self-pity or laziness. These are all common temptations that we feel as humans, but there is good news in the gospel of Jesus Christ. Temptations are common to mankind; they are not unique; God has already provided you an out—a way of escape so that they do not overtake you. Whatever it is that you are battling, know that God does not expect you to handle these issues on your own. You have the power of the Holy Spirit living inside of you and you just have to tap into that power in order to overcome temptations.

Sure, sometimes the Holy Spirit may be leading you to find additional support such as group programs, counseling, or pastoral/spiritual help. However, you must realize that you aren't helpless and weak over your temptations. Once you begin to speak the word of God over your temptations, and believe that word, meaning that you digest it, repeat it, and declare it to yourself daily, you will gain the inner strength needed to resist and overcome. Never forget that God gives a way of escape. He does not leave you hanging. He is a GOOD GOOD FATHER! That right there is a reason to rejoice. It is important that you understand your authority and power in Christ and over your temptations. Drugs, sex, alcohol, a toxic relationship, a toxic job, or bad habits do not control you. You control them.

Today we encourage you to meditate on this scripture and apply it to your life. Replace "temptation" with your specific issue, and speak life over those things.

It's time to walk into your FOREVER, and the enemy no longer has control over these areas of your life. Today is the day that you take back your control and take inheritance of all the possessions God has for you and everything the enemy tried to steal.

Pray:

Dear God, I have fallen victim to these temptations in the past. But today, I stand on your word, which says no temptation has overtaken me except such as is common to man; but YOU are faithful, and you will not allow me to be tempted beyond what I can handle. With this temptation, you have promised me a way of escape, Lord. Today, I give these temptations to you, and I ask for you strength. Fight my battles for me, and I will stand strong behind your shield of protection. I know through you all things are possible Lord, and I have complete faith that I am more than a conqueror through you Christ Jesus. Thank you for loving me, saving me, and rescuing me from a life of sin. I love you. In Jesus' name, I pray, AMEN.

Day 14

*Write:*_____

List any areas of temptations and struggles, and ask God to give you strength and a way out. Commit those areas to the Lord through writing and prayer. Take note of this day, and return to your journal to document your answered prayers.

_____

_____

_____

_____

_____

_____

_____

_____

_____

_____

_____

_____

_____

_____

_____

_____

_____

_____

We pray that you enjoyed *God Made Me Wait*. We encourage you to return to the devotions and the thoughts that you shared with God in the journals to track your growth and remind yourself of your personal commitments and God's promises to you. We love you always,

Sherrell & Natasha

Please leave a review on Amazon. Visit ForeverDuncan.com/books to order additional books by Sherrell & Alfred Duncan and Sherrell and Natasha T. Brown.

Follow Sherrell:

@SherrellTheTrainer on Instagram and Periscope

Sherrell Duncan on Facebook

Follow Natasha:

@NatashaTBrown on Instagram, Twitter, and Periscope

Natasha T. Brown on Facebook

Sherrell & Alfred Duncan's book will be released in 2017.

Stay up-to-date with ForeverDuncan.com for all things

#ForeverDuncan.

About the Authors

Sherrell Duncan is a former model and agency owner, who was well-known in the DC nightlife. In 2010, she became a depressed, emotional eater and alcoholic after the birth of her first child. She gained over 90 pounds after her daughter was born, making her over 300 pounds. Due to being overweight, she developed high blood pressure, high cholesterol, suffered from heart palpitations and chronic headaches. Her life changed on January 4, 2013 when she had a minor heart attack scare at work. She was rushed to the hospital to learn that her weight was the cause of her health complications. She began seeing a trainer and a nutritionist. She completely turned her life around and decided to eat clean and workout daily.

Sherrell created The Good Thick, LLC in October of 2013. Now, as a full-time, self employed Certified Health Advisor, Sherrell and The Good Thick offers a plethora of products, personal health training, weight loss plans, nutritional tips, and a Queens Empowerment Hour bible study. She has loss 101 pounds following The Good Thick plan and has coached her female clientele-base of nearly 50 women to their weight loss goals. Sherrell's story is an inspiration to women who have felt hopeless in their weight loss goals, and have battled with self-esteem, depression and health issues as a result. Her life's mission is to inspire total body transformations.

On October 1, 2016, Sherrell married the love of her life Alfred Duncan, and their wedding inspired the world. Now, through the #ForeverDuncan movement, she serves as a relationship mentor, speaker and author alongside of her husband. **God Made Me Wait** is Sherrell's debut book.

Natasha Brown coaches trauma survivors and entrepreneurs from tragedy to strategy. She is a Communicator for Christ, Best Selling Author and Ghostwriter who inspires audiences young and old with a testimony of faith, resilience and a determination to win.

As the founder of 10 Blessings Inspiration, Inc., a 501 (c)3 non-profit organization, co-founder of Brown & Duncan Brand, LLC, and the creator of the Blessed-Branded-Brilliant Entrepreneur Society, Natasha helps visionaries repurpose their past into books, brands, missions and ministries. In 2015, Natasha published *10 Blessings of Betrayal,* a bestselling self-help memoir about her journey of healing and triumph after surviving false accusations and domestic violence. Through her non-profit 10 Blessings Inspiration, she formed the 10K Survivors Domestic Violence Coalition of survivors throughout the United States who help victims break free.

Natasha earned a bachelor's degree in communications from Morgan State University, a master's degree in professional writing from Towson University and is now pursuing a master's of divinity degree from Regent University. Natasha is the author/ghostwriter of over 15 books.

Made in the USA
Charleston, SC
16 December 2016